THE JOURNEY'S ECHO

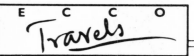

E C C O

Travels

The Journey's Echo

Selections from

FREYA STARK

FOREWORD BY LAWRENCE DURRELL

THE ECCO PRESS

New York

First published in 1988 by The Ecco Press
26 West 17th Street, New York, NY 10011
Published simultaneously in Canada by
Penguin Books Canada Ltd., Ontario
Printed in the United States of America
Cover by Beth Tondreau Design
Published by arrangement with John Murray Publishers Ltd.

The publisher wishes to thank Coward-McCann, Inc. for permission
to use material from The Freya Stark Story, by Freya Stark, copy-
right 1950, 1951, 1953 by Freya Stark; and Beacon Press for material
from Perseus in the Wind

Library of Congress Cataloging-in-Publication Data

Stark, Freya.
The journey's echo:
selections from Freya Stark / foreword by Lawrence Durrell.
p.   cm.   —   (Ecco travels)
Reprint. Originally published: London: J. Murray, 1963.
1. Middle East—Description and travel.
2. Stark, Freya—Journeys—Middle East.
I. Title.   II. Series.
DS49.S756 1988   915.6´043—dc19   88–16344

ISBN 0-88001-218-8

This book, the idea of which I owe to others, could not have been published without the kind and assiduous care of Mr. John Gibbins. To him, and to Mrs. Deuchar and Mr. John Grey Murray, as well as to Mr. Lawrence Durrell my warmest thanks are due.

F.S.

Contents

Foreword

The observations and impressions gathered together in this book have been selected from the writings of one of the most remarkable women of our age – a poet of travel whose Muse has been wholly Arabian in plumage and whose books span nearly half a century of historical time.

They seem to burn on the page, these thoughtfully chosen paragraphs (so often with their sharply aphoristic turn which reminds one of Arab proverbs); burning like those small fires of thorn-scrub which the travelling beduin light at night upon the desert's dark floors; fires which give off an even, temperate signal-flame and heat enough for a night meal during a forced march. And when the fires die down their embers lie long under the ash, banking easily for the use of other travellers along the same trail.

Presented thus – in little sips, so to speak, – the new reader can appreciate more fully the magnitude and range of Freya Stark's achievement while those who have long known and admired her work will once more be reminded of the singular qualities of heart and mind which inform it. They are choice ones indeed and doubly to be treasured in an age which has begun to despise them – an age in which the tourist has replaced the traveller. A whole range of sympathies and insights is necessary if we are to interpret foreign nations to ourselves as she has done so lucidly in her books. But over and above such gifts of unusual sensibility there must be something else – a quality which might seem paradoxical. A great traveller (in distinction to a merely good one) is a kind of introspective; as she covers the ground outwardly, so she advances towards fresh interpretations of herself inwardly. And this is the quality which lends Freya Stark's books the memorable poetic density which is their special *cachet*. Moreover, it is this quality which makes them as fresh and striking today as the day on which they were first penned; this is what will preserve them when so much of today's prose is forgotten. Her work is full of echoes.

To interpret foreign lands with philosophic awareness and detachment, to record and compare faithfully, to muse with felicity on the meaning of history – all these things are within the gift of this noble author. Her books have already taken their place on the high shelves among the great names which range from Purchas to Doughty and Lawrence. Her qualities will keep them there. But this small anthology is by design both a celebration of her past work and an earnest of the work to come. The lucky reader who comes fresh to her is much to be envied; I can think of nothing more exciting than to stumble for the first time (and if possible purely by hazard) upon prose so melodious, so energetic and so spare.

LAWRENCE DURRELL

and publicizing research.

While some therapies have been studied extensively, the report notes that "no critical mass of researchers, clinicians and policy makers has formed to give them more exposure and recognition."

But Trachtenberg says the report will be distributed at NIH "to seed people's interest," and even sent to medical schools. "I think this represents the field of alternative medicine coming of age," he says.

The public can order the report ($25) from the Government Printing Office; call 202-512-1800 for details.

USTOMERS

Federal
e effective on March

Option Y, mainland

arge which will apply
Billed Account having
s subscribed to AT&T.
n Billed Account are
amount to meet the

On Marc
USADirec
filed for A
0.6%. Rate
Calling Pl
across all
on April

The affec
Armenia,
Belize, Be
Verde Isla
Islands, C
Republic,
Finland, F
Greece, G
Israel, Ivo
Kyrgyzsta
Macedoni
Montserra
Federal R
Portugal,
Singapore
Sweden, S
Turkey, T
Venezuela

move your feet

An Alphabet of
DINOSAURS

BY PETER DODSON • PAINTINGS BY WAYNE D. BARLOWE

vary f
Home)
Circus
includ
If I H
dred
(pric
dling
Bo

***Train Songs &
Other Tracks,*** by
Kevin Roth (Mari-
boro Records, cas-
sette $10.98; CD
$15.98, all ages).
Kids who watch PBS' *Shining Time
Station* will recognize Kevin Roth's
voice — he sings the theme song,
included in this collection of 15
songs primarily about trains. Tunes

with this
makes h
dlers. Ch
leads six
through
Set to or
tap again
at the po
jazz at th
els and
are reh
all toget

Donahue

To awaken quite alone in a strange town is one of the pleasant sensations in the world. You are surrounded by adventure. You have no idea of what is in store for you, but you will, if you are wise and know the art of travel, let yourself go on the stream of the unknown and accept whatever comes in the spirit in which the gods may offer it. For this reason your customary thoughts, all except the rarest of your friends, even most of your luggage—everything, in fact, which belongs to your everyday life, is merely a hindrance. The tourist travels in his own atmosphere like a snail in his shell and stands, as it were, on his own perambulating doorstep to look at the continents of the world. But if you discard all this, and sally forth with a leisurely and blank mind, there is no knowing what may not happen to you.

BAGHDAD SKETCHES

Letters from Syria

1927–8

We are now among islands in the Ionian Sea. . . . The sea is quiet, the twilight falling. I asked for the name of an island on the right. 'Ithaca,' says the Captain, as if the name were mere geography. And there it is, with a hill rising sheer, and a little sandy cove and village above, cypresses and olives, bare and poor; and Penelope no doubt in the square villa with the well-kept garden. Islands on islands there are, melting away into the night. They are all incredibly steep, many with great cliffs, and wild land at the back, bare ranges. One can see the early adventurers, slipping on from one inlet to the next, as we would turn the corners of a road, in this landlocked sea.

❖   ❖   ❖

It was lovely country, and a windy day with shadows. As Rhodes is small, it seems to have made up its mind to condense all sorts of landscape in a narrow space. We ran through dry poor lands, thin olives here and there and neither shade nor water; down into orange groves, and fruit trees and long grass; and then into Macchia, among small pines, and cypress of the kind outspread like cedars, and climbed up on to a high rocky ridge, the island backbone, among cool fir woods, old lichen-covered trees where the air struck cold. The anemones are in bloom, both the white and the bloodstained ones of the legend; and leaves everywhere of asphodel and narcissus. And all is absolutely lonely. The peasants live shut up in villages, which you come upon with startling suddenness, glittering white, low and flat-roofed like clusters of boxes.

❖   ❖   ❖

The whole place is a most amusing mixture of Europe smeared thin on a whole depth of primitive life below. Even the landscape is like this with the perfect barbaric glory of its sunsets and its grand lines not laid out for peaceful friendly life, and then the neat villages built as tidily as toys. And you admire the little square houses and ask why so many of them are allowed to stand about roofless and windowless, and are told that these belonged to people who died of hunger during the war. And so it all is – life and death side by side with a suddenness which gives a good barbaric flavour.   LEBANON

       ❖   ❖   ❖

I found three red anemones: then we eked them out with the deep crimson poppies that stand in the grass along the lower reaches of the stream and climbed up on to the Roman bridge, which is the shape of a rainbow. We flung the flowers down and watched them float away like rubies in the sun on the green water . . . and the first Adonis has had for a long time I expect. And it was pleasant to see the Syrian Headmaster of a Missionary School sacrificing to his ancestral gods.   LEBANON

       ❖   ❖   ❖

There is an emancipated feeling with a car that will wander over cornfields: it ceases to be a machine.

       ❖   ❖   ❖

What I find trying in a country which you do not understand and where you cannot speak, is that you can never be *yourself*. You are English, or Christian, or Protestant, or anything but your individual *you*: and whatever you say or do is fitted to the label and burdened with whatever misdeeds (or good deeds) your predecessors may have committed. And then of course your sentences, intended with just the shade of meaning you desire, come out shorn of all accessories, quite useless for anything except the mere procuring of bread and butter. How glad I shall be when I can feel that the country is really *mine*, not the mere panorama to the stranger. Meanwhile the world is open. I feel that my seven years' patience is rewarded with Rebecca straightaway, and am very happy.

       ❖   ❖   ❖

The method of strengthening people by starvation and murder seems absurd, but there is no doubt it appears to work here. They are as hardy as can be. When you think of them as compared to Italy, it is like thinking of iron and earthenware: you feel these people are hard *all through*. I imagine that what is wrong with them is just what was wrong with their Phoenician ancestors: they have no imagination; therefore no ideals, or not sufficient to make them really do something.   BRUMANA

❖   ❖   ❖

Another thing I have noticed is the absolute lack of all historical sense among these people. No *perspective*. What happened five hundred years ago has the exact vividness of yesterday. It came upon me with a shock when a child here was reading out some of the more gruesome massacres in Kings: I decided on the spot that I should leave the Old Testament out of the curriculum if I were a missionary, and stick to Christian charity and the New. If you come to think of it, the Old Testament is the worst literature possible for these races: with that on the one hand and the Koran on the other the reign of toleration has very little chance.   DAMASCUS

❖   ❖   ❖

It was good walking in the solitude with the cyclamen and blue anemones blossoming all to themselves in little glades. The valleys go up steep as stairs from their river beds till you reach the first shelf: then up from shelf to shelf of good wide, level ground, till you find mulberry patches, and vines and villages on the third or fourth ledge where the sun can shine all day. There are no people down below except wood-cutters and charcoal burners. Now and then in the stillness you hear their axes and look and look till something gleams and moves among the tufts of trees and grey rocks. I don't believe even the winds get down into these deep valleys. One feels as if one were surprising a secret as one goes down – and it is almost as

pleasant to come up again and meet the first cows or
donkeys browsing about on the other side.   LEBANON

❖   ❖   ❖

The valley suddenly opened, and there in the afternoon
sun was Damascus, yellow as an opal, the river running
through between straight banks like a willow-pattern
plate. There is the exact description in Chaucer somewhere, of Simois 'like an arrow clere' flowing through
Troy, and I thought of it as I came along, and before
the railway station turned the East to mere untidiness.

❖   ❖   ❖

Immensity of size is impressive . . . and one *feels* the
size too, acting harmoniously like strength. There is one
beautiful square door immensely high. The temple inside
is nearly perfect too, all but the roof; and there the little
hawks were flying with shrill cries and black outlines of
feathers clear round their white bodies – or they looked
white against the blue. Swallows, and hawks, and lizards,
and little far figures of tourists clambering: all small busy
lives running among these ruins, which seemed to belong
to the land itself rather than to anything human in it: as
if the worship of Baal and Helios and Jupiter, and then
Theodosius's temple; and then the Moslem walls, were all
inherent secrets.   BAALBEK

❖   ❖   ❖

But even the glories of Baalbek have no joy to give like
this of discovering your own ruins among the quiet fields
and streets, coming upon them unregarded though even
here dominant in their unrecognized loveliness.

❖   ❖   ❖

The light is so lovely, so pure and brilliant: one feels
it here as St. Augustine saw it, 'that Queen of colours'.
There is nothing on these naked hills to interfere with its
lovely play, and they change like water with the reflections
of the sky.   ❖   ❖   ❖

6

Yesterday, as I came from a walk through a little group of houses, I was invited in (they always do this). I was glad of the rest, too. The rooms were beautifully clean; stone floors and straw mats. In one corner a new yellow and white quilt and a head all wrapped in bandages (I thought). The lady of the house went up and shook the protesting head from its sleep. I couldn't tell whether it was a man or a woman, but asked whether it was wounded.

'Oh no,' said the lady, much surprised, 'she is the mother of a baby,'' and there in the cradle, so covered that not a breath of air could touch her, was a two-day-old baby girl. 'Another one here,' said the grandmother, lifting a far corner of the quilt and rolling out a child. 'And another here,' turning over what seemed to be a small bolster. I sat contemplating from the divan, feeling as one does in the presence of the conjurer who manufactures rabbits, and not knowing what to say. Three girls one on top of another is a real calamity to a poor young wife. 'You must be happy with your "bint",' says I inadequately at last. 'You can take one away with you,' says the mother, suddenly arousing herself to animation.

LEBANON

❖   ❖   ❖

It is a leisurely land. Everyone has time to talk, everyone is ready to be interested: it is only when you want to get anything done that you begin to be unhappy. To buy a dressing-gown is pure Romance. You sit on the ledge of a little shop and the merchant spreads his wares: an audience gathers, and advises: the money-changer comes along to help. Then you bargain. You are told that the thought of profit does not enter with One whose face is like the Moon: whereupon you offer half. Then the diplomatic merchant says that he knows you are 'a daughter of the Arabs'; and who would refuse him anything after that?   DAMASCUS

❖   ❖   ❖

I can't help feeling pleased through all the discomfort at living as it were among real things; the sun not a mere ornament in the heavens, but something on which your day's happiness depends; and the Spring looked forward to with all the feelings which you find in the old writers before the days of comfortable houses.

❖　❖　❖

Delicious sleep in a tent; with the camels tethered outside, and the gentle flap of the hair cloth in the night wind; the sense of great spaces around us, and silence and the nearness of the stars.　　　　　JEBEL DRUSE

❖　❖　❖

After we had sat a long time on the roof, and more men had gathered round us, we were invited down to the court of the house, where two camels and our three donkeys were tied to the enclosing yellow mud wall. There was a low platform against the house, and they had spread us a carpet and a pile of cushions for our elbows, and we sat and watched the pot cooking over a fire indoors, and the women with long white veils wrapped well over the mouth walking to and fro with their beautiful barefoot walk, attending to the supper, carrying little oil lights as the night darkened, and looking like so many Tanagra figures moving noiselessly. It was very wonderful; and quiet: the animals munching peacefully with a little tinkle of bells now and then: two small pomegranate trees in flower over the top of the wall against the western sky.

When it grew quite late and dark we were conducted into a big whitewashed room with a fire in an open fireplace in the corner and carpets spread for us all – six men besides our party. We took off our shoes, and they put a round basket mat before us, and leban, rice, olives, cheese and eggs in little dishes. We were their first European visitors. They gave us spoons, but we preferred to try scooping our dinner up with the bread and caused much pleasure and amusement. It was all beautifully clean –

very different from Damascus. The women waited on us. Dogs, cats and children came as near as they dared.

❖   ❖   ❖

The Druses really have much better manners. I am not sure that the fact of keeping the women as such absolute inferiors does not help to give the men their remarkable dignity: even the poorest always has someone in his own house on whom to practise the manners of a king, and so the grand air comes natural. I am not saying the game is worth the candle, but the manner is certainly there and very pleasant to find. The Druses have only one wife, and if they divorce her they can never change their minds and marry her again, as the Moslems may do.

❖   ❖   ❖

We were very tired. I felt broken to bits, and very glad when they took us out to sleep. There was a murmured consultation as to whether there would be too many bugs for us indoors: 'They are not accustomed,' said Najm anxiously. I pretended not to listen but was very decidedly in favour of a bed in the open when the suggestion was made. They spread our platform with mattresses and quilts; we looked up into the sky full of white clouds, and pools of stars; and were very happy. When the moon rose I woke up and saw the two camels padding out from Deir Ali on their way to reach Damascus at dawn. It seemed incredible that this was really I! It was not exactly comfortable; there was a sort of hill under my mattress which began to move in the middle of the night, and turned out to be 'Arif, the small nephew: it must have been worse for him than for me, but after all I had not asked him to settle with all me and my bed on top of him. As for fleas, Keating's has succumbed to numbers.

❖   ❖   ❖

There was a grey sky, and an arid hot wind from the west. We came by a lonely waterhole; three riders were there talking to sitters by the well, the long tails of the horses and the leader's bright green cloak swishing about in the wind. They kindly wheeled about to let me take a picture. The man in green was the Sheikh of Imtune, the next village: he went off like a centaur, his beautiful little Arab picking its way among the stones.   JEBEL DRUSE

❖   ❖   ❖

This is wild country, full of ruined stones and cities, a sad beauty of its own over its greyness. Here you reckon time from Sunrise to Sunset. You greet hastily on the road to see if it is to be Peace, if your greeting is returned. Life has the charm of being secured at a cost of personal endeavour, a thing sweet because not valued too highly. That surely is freedom.   JEBEL DRUSE

❖   ❖   ❖

Black tents were dotted round. It was a happy place; open sky and the river moving slowly, quite deep, through the grassy plain. The beduin came towards us and we strolled to the tents. I think I was well inspired: I asked for the sheikh's tent, and this seemed to be the right thing: it was the biggest of them all, open along the front and divided into wattled compartments, and we were taken to the largest compartment where the two coffee pots stood in a hole in the ground and the sheikh himself lay fast asleep beside them. In a corner at one end all the tiny lambs were huddled safely.

A rug was spread for us: we squatted down, and looked across at our sleeping host, who began to come to himself very gradually. Mr. Edmunds considers that he did it with great dignity, but I was feeling slightly nervous as to my unsupported Arabic (M. Paul knows a few words, but they usually say something he doesn't intend). The sheikh finally came to a sitting posture, in which he remained meditative for a while with his eyes on the ground, looking magnificent in his flowing garments and grey beard. He then spat, reached out a hand to the man nearest him – a fierce long-faced Arab with two long pigtails – and began murmuring in quite incomprehensible language which did not sound particularly cordial. I made a feeble attempt at explaining our existence, but one can't carry on small talk with a Patriarch, and the correct thing seemed to be to sit silent, which we did for some time.

After a long while, the sheikh stretched his hand to the coffee pot, and poured out a few sips into two little cups which he handed to me and M. Paul (I was surprised at the woman being first served!). Another problem: was one to drink it all, or leave some in the cup? One ought to know these formalities before wandering. I left some, and seemed to have done the wrong thing, for the sheikh looked at it with awful intentness and finally poured it away on the ground, and gave me no more; which was a pity, for it was so good. M. Paul then offended very seriously by refusing the cigarette which the kind A.D.C. had (literally) just licked into shape for him. He made it up by offering his tobacco pouch, and the atmosphere began to thaw. 'Oh daughter of my heart,' said the old sheikh to some question of mine; after that I felt all must be well. NEAR DAMASCUS

❖   ❖   ❖

Camels appeared on our left hand: first a few here and there, then more and more till the whole herd came browsing along, five hundred or more. I got out and went among them to photograph. The two beduin leaders, dressed gorgeously, perched high up and swinging slowly with the movement of their beasts, shouted out to me, but the beduin Arabic is beyond me. I can't tell you what a wonderful sight it was: as if one were suddenly in the very morning of the world among the people of Abraham or Jacob. The great gentle creatures came browsing and moving and pausing, rolling gently over the landscape like a brown wave just a little browner than the desert that carried it. Their huge legs rose up all round me like columns; the foals were frisking about: the herdsmen rode here and there. I stood in a kind of ecstasy among them. It seemed as if they were not so much moving as flowing along, with something indescribably fresh and peaceful and free about it all, as if the struggle of all these thousands of years had never been, since first they started wandering. I never imagined that my first sight of the desert would come with such a shock of beauty and enslave me right away.   NEAR DAMASCUS

⬦   ⬦   ⬦

After a while all the men stood up for a dance. They called a handsome bedu maid from the women's side of the tent, and dressed her in one of the men's great cloaks and stood in a close row behind her clapping their hands with the long waving white sleeves and giving short low growls, very staccato and incredibly fierce, while the girl sailed up and down in front of them with a little stick in one hand and a handkerchief in the other, the clumsy garment billowing out like a sail, the movements slow and graceful: and the men all bent towards her, the whole line swaying this way and that as she moved, the clapping and growling keeping time together but growing faster and sharper, and faster and sharper, their wild faces half hidden under the dark kafiyehs, the eyes shining out and the long dirty sleeves dancing like streamers.

JEBEL DRUSE

⬦   ⬦   ⬦

I saw a bedu waving to his horse and the creature come to him from quite a distance, galloping, a beautiful sight. If you wave your sleeve (they wear very long trailing ones), it is a sign of friendship: this man made us the signal, a draped figure standing in that loneliness as our car jolted over the rough ground. One can hardly believe all this is Real Life and not mere Literature! We found a Roman fort, nothing of it left but walls, still square and sharp, the big stones laid without mortar, the waste lands round it. Behind us and already out of sight ran the last eastern road, old as the Druids and trodden always by people on the watch: no peaceful harvests or leisurely strolling there. The wind was howling and buffeting, with clouds scudding along, making the landscape soft as a moorland, though it was nothing but wormwood and baked earth. We ate our food with little clouds of Roman sand blown off the hewn stones and thought of the fragility of things. NEAR DAMASCUS

◇ ◇ ◇

Our poor donkeys stumbled about, very tired; we had done seven and a half hours that day. Just before it got quite dark we clattered through the Roman gate, half ruined, and found a broad Roman street, its houses in heaps on either hand. Our hoofs rang on the pavement: it was as if we entered among ghosts. We came to where the triumphal arch once stood, at the crossing of two great streets, and went uphill, past three temple columns. White-turbaned Druses were sitting at the doorsteps. It was as if all the centuries were whispering behind them. We knocked at the door we had been told of, and the women welcomed us, and made us rest in a charming yellow room – always the same ochre wash – decorated with paintings and the bright round mats all hung along the walls. SHAHBA, JEBEL DRUSE

◇ ◇ ◇

We went and sat outside on the long seat by the door while the young men of the village drew themselves up in a line to dance before us – a long semicircle rather – with the lantern on the ground throwing its light up at them, and one youth whose hand-clapping led the chorus: his head-dress had come off and his head was shaven halfway up with about a dozen little plaits dangling all round, and he led very skilfully, singing one verse of a long long chant – a marriage song, I think. The clapping hands all kept time, and the whole gathering took up the refrain, eight syllables, always the same: at intervals they would break off into the dance we had seen among the beduin, only far wilder, for it was now one or other of the men who would leave his place and come into the middle of the circle, and stand there jerking his body like an epileptic with little rigid jerks all up and down the line, facing the others and clapping furiously, and rousing those opposite him to a perfect frenzy of clapping and growling; then he would dash at one of them and tear off his head-dress, and this man would come into the middle while the other went back into the swaying clapping line; the growls were scarce human; it was like some primitive rage inexpressible in words. The jumping figure in front was indescribably evil, the long gown and flying hair, and frenzy of passion, bent nearly double to urge the others on. The growling and clapping grew faster and faster; the line swayed as one man; the light flickered over them against the black of the night; one could not watch without a sort of terror, as if something unknown and appalling were suddenly finding its voice.   JEBEL DRUSE

Baghdad Sketches

1929

The desert lies in front; not sand, but hard red earth, with beds of flints strewn over its low heights. The camels of the Rualla, in dun-coloured herds, drift here in hundreds over its green fringe. That comes to an end, and presently there is nothing, not even thin spikes of grey grasses in the hollows. White sheets of mirage, like a shallow lake country far away, melt in the horizon, run into each other, recede as we approach. The land curves gently, in waves so smooth, it is as if each easy rise were but the rounded bosom of the earth, each gentle dip but her soft movement as she slips through space; and the hours go with nothing to count them by but the fierce steps of the sun, the Lord Absolute in his own land.

◇   ◇   ◇

Everything we could see around was young and fresh and enchanted with the fact of being alive. And there were not too many things to see round us, as there are in most landscapes: there was only the desert, green and new, on which our black colony of tents floated like a school of porpoises on a quiet sea. Baby donkeys, fluffy and mouse-coloured, gambolled about. Kids and lambs, separated from their parents, were sent off in nurseries by themselves with some diminutive shepherd in a striped abba to look after them. The Arab babies, with blue beads wherever possible and nothing on in the way of under-clothing, rolled in and out of their tents; while, in some unobtrusive corner where stones might not be thrown, even the py-dogs had puppies, and added to the unwanted population of the world.

◇   ◇   ◇

I like these slow yellow streams. As they silt up or shift in their lazy beds, they remove cities bodily from one district to another. They are as indolent and wayward, powerful, beneficient, and unpitying as the Older Gods whom no doubt they represent: and there is no greater desolation in this land than to come upon their dry beds, long abandoned, but still marked step by step with sand-coloured ruins of the desert.

❖   ❖   ❖

The width of the Tigris in Baghdad is about four hundred yards, a noble stream. It is the only sweet and fresh thoroughfare of the town: not clear water, but lion-coloured, like Tiber or Arno. Its broad flowing surface is dyed by the same earth of which the houses and minarets on its banks are built, so that all is one tawny harmony. Its low winter mists in early morning, or yellow slabs of sunset shallows when the water buffaloes come down to drink after the day; its many craft, evolved through the centuries so that one looks as it were upon an epitome of the history of ships from the earliest days of mankind; the barefoot traffic of its banks, where the women come with jars upon their shoulders and boatmen tow their vessels against the current; all this was a perpetual joy in my new home.

❖   ❖   ❖

It is always strange and like a dream to walk in star-light among the narrower ways ... but now in Ra-madhan it is fantastic. The whole city rustles and moves and whispers in its labyrinthine alleys like a beehive swarming in the dark. One cannot distinguish faces; the murmuring figures glide by like flowing water paying scant attention to the anomaly of a European in their midst at this late hour. The extraordinary unity of Islam comes over me. These crowds are moving through all the cities of the East: from Morocco to Afghanistan, from Turkey to India and Java, they walk abroad through the nights of the Fast. In their shadows they are dim and unreal, less clear to the eye of the imagination than that Arabian Merchant who first set them in motion twelve centuries ago. How firmly he pressed his finger into the clay of the world! So that these sheeplike figures still obey, moving hither and thither in the night; and make one think, marvelling at its range of mediocrity and splendour, of the power of the mind and will of man.

BAGHDAD

❖ ❖ ❖

To sit there among the pressed houses, so crowded within the security of their wall that there was scarcely room in front of the mosque for the little stone-flagged square, was to realize what for several thousand years of our history has constituted the feeling of safety, the close-packed enclosure of small cities crammed within walls. Outside are the wilderness, or the neighbouring unfriendly cities, or the raiding deserts; inside the intimacy where strangers or dissenters are watched with fear or anger. And from the outer suburbs that swell or shrink in times of peace or war, this intimate sense of safety or seclusion grows and grows – through the dark bazaars, and the taller clustering houses, through the courtyard and into the last inner sanctity of the shrine itself.*

NEJF, IRAQ

❖ ❖ ❖

My neighbour points with her cigarette to a rather grim dowager who is leaving the room. 'My husband's first wife,' she tells me.

'Do you see much of her?' I ask.

'We meet in the houses of our friends. We are related.'

'It must be hard for the first wife, in the beginning,' I venture.

The ladies near by smile indulgently. A careless husband, they seem to think, is not so trying as a bad digestion, which is what the next group is discussing. Both are dispensations of providence, over which they have not much control. There is some point, I reflect, in being

* From 'The Golden Domes of Iraq and Iran', *Cornhill Magazine*, Spring 1961.

19

able to shove one's husband into the region of the Inevitable and the Uncontrollable; he ceases to be a worry,
just like one's unsatisfactory profile, or anything else that
one has not had a hand in the making of and cannot
alter. Perhaps that is why the older ladies look so peaceful.
'Life is like that,' one of them is saying philosophically.

⋄ ⋄ ⋄

'And so,' says my neighbour with the charming smile,
'when she saw that her husband would pay no attention
to her, she used to put pepper every night into the baby's
eyes, and its wailing filled the house so that it became a
nuisance even in the new wife's lodging in the next court.
At last it grew so impossible that the husband himself
came to her apartment to see what was the matter; and
when another baby was born in the course of time, she
insisted on calling it "Pepper". But none of the men of
the family know the reason to this day.'

⋄ ⋄ ⋄

Whether these Western floods, to which all her sluices
are open, come to the East for baptism or drowning, is
hard to say. Total immersion in any case she is bound to
submit to and we – who love the creature – wait with
some misgiving to see in what condition her regenerated
head will reappear above the waters; we stand upon the
shore and collect such oddments as we find floating in
chaos – her customs, religions, her clothes and trinkets
and some, alas! of her virtues. We snatch them as they
drift for ever out of sight, and encase them in an armour
of words – and by so doing, not unhopeful of the future,
yet wage our little losing battle against the fragilities of
Time.

⋄ ⋄ ⋄

In early spring, before the first buds show on the peach
trees, a sort of luminous transparency envelops the distant
city of Baghdad and its gardens. The pale minarets, the
slowly swelling river, the desert itself with darker patches

20

where fields of beetroot lie near the irrigation ditches, the russet lace-work of the willows so frail against the sky – all take on an ethereal quality, as of some faint angelic vision about to melt into its own heavenly atmosphere, some fugitive embrace of earth and sky which has left this print of loveliness behind it for the eyes of men. The blue domes melt into a heaven of their own colour; the palm trees, bleached and pale after the winter, let the sun lie quiet as moonlight on their spiky polished crowns; and everywhere there is the voice of doves, sleepy and gentle . . . and soft as the grey feathers which slip between palm and palm, or settle in crooning clouds on every cupola.

Nothing is loud, nothing is garish, except young blades of the autumn-sown corn . . . among the mongeese, under the columnar stems of the palms in the late afternoon. They catch the light and shine brilliant as haloes not yet cut out into circles – so much more vivid than any mere terrestial object has the right to be.

Before it has attained to this glory, and while yet the harmony of soft tones is unbroken, the spring has come; and all the lands that seemed so dead and dun around the city are filled with the bent figures of peasants, squatting over the ditches, squatting over the beetroots and lettuces, over the low brushwood screens that protect their plants from the north wind. They are anchored to the earth to which they belong, and seem unable to separate themselves from it even to the extent of standing up straight on their two feet; they squat on their hams with a small sickle in their hand even to the cutting of their hay.

❖　❖　❖

I suppose that, after the passion of love, water rights have caused more trouble than anything else to the human species. Our word for rival, or rivalry, comes from the Latin *riva* – the bank or margin of a stream – and the justice of the derivation is proved at any rate in Iraq.

❖　❖　❖

We were out under the stars, with shapes of palm trees moving against the blue night sky. And suddenly, as if standing alone in space, the tops of the four gilt minarets of the Holy City appeared, illuminated by the lights at their summits which shine through all the nights of Ramadhan. A row of small green and red and yellow lights below enclosed the square of the shrine: the two golden domes gleamed here and there, almost invisible in the shadow of the night. The deep sky behind, the half-lighted building, the carriage full of pilgrims in their dim abstraction, had a strange solemnity: the surrounding darkness hid all the ugliness and squalor which ever comes near beauty in the East.   KADHIMAIN

❖   ❖   ❖

The magic of the Holy Cities indeed is difficult now to recapture, since the element that so largely made it was the element of Time. Combustion engines of one sort and another have taken it away: and though the actual view across steppe or desert has not greatly altered, the feeling has changed since those who leave a hotel in Baghdad or Teheran can see the domes of the sanctuaries floating on the selfsame day in their pale skies. Preparation is lacking. The pilgrim, when he walked across those emptinesses that led to his desire – or even if he was rich enough to sway day after day towards it on a camel – had already, as it were, appropriated the golden vision into his dreams. It had been described to him many times in small and remote places by those who had made the long and arduous journey before him. From the Elburz mountains of north-west Iran to Kerbela, or to Nejf in its black walls (now demolished) people, whom I myself have spoken to, have taken a good month on the way. The stages were marked by philanthropic forbears – Zobeide, the Queen of the Caliph Harun-ar-Rashid is still kindly remembered. In the desert, by some poor waters, at an easy eight-hour or so camel distance one from the other, the square blank walls of the *khans* dissolve with their lonely gateways tumbled in a heap. They gape to empty courtyards where the nights are now solitary and the sun is the only traveller; and the single-storeyed compartments that surround the inside walls, with flattened curves cushioned against the sky – the inner room for the merchant with a door to close it, and the outer pillared space for his own animals to munch beside him within earshot through the night – these too have fallen silent, filled only with the clean and living desert air.*

❖   ❖   ❖

All through the ten days of 'Ashura the Shi'as in Islam mourn for the death of Husain, until the slow mounting tide of their grief reaches its climax with the last processions, and the slain body itself is carried under a blood-stained sheet through wailing crowds, where the red headdress of the Sunni is well advised not to make itself conspicuous. All is represented, every incident of the fatal day of Kerbela; and the procession stops at intervals to act one episode or other in a little clearing of the crowd. One can hear it coming from far away by the thud of the beaters beating their naked chests, a mighty sound like the beating of carpets; or see the blood pour down the backs of those who acquire merit with flails made of knotted chains with which they lacerate their shoulders, bared for the purpose: and when the body itself comes, headless (the man's head is hidden in a box and a small boy with a fan walks beside it to prevent suffocation), its two feet sticking out of the bloody drapery, the truncated neck of a sheep protruding at the other end, a dagger cunningly stuck above each shoulder into the cloth – when this comes heaving through the crowd, there is such a passion of anger and sorrow, such a wailing of women from the roofs, such glances of repulsion towards the foreigner who happens to be looking on, that it is quite understandable that the civilized governments of the East

  * From 'The Golden Domes of Iraq and Iran', *Cornhill Magazine,* Spring 1961.

are now doing all they can to discourage this expression of religion in favour of forms more liturgical.

❖ ❖ ❖

It was a small court, with two pointed arches at one end, of whitewashed mud and straw, roughly decorated. Old awnings prolonged the shade in patches half across the open space, and at the upper end, under the twilight of the arches, black cloth was nailed around with little squares of cardboard in sign of mourning. Here, with a green satin banner behind them, stood the four ladies who conducted the ceremony, chanting their parts, repeating one line over and over before they went on to the next, and bobbing with every verse to the congregation, which rose and bobbed in return like a wave, diminishing toward the outer distance.

One wondered, as one watched, into what dim prehistoric days this monotonous chant might lead one, back and back through the recesses of time. The four Readers, unconscious of being observed, stood as if drugged with dull pain while they beat their breasts. They were all different in type – the nearest handsome like a Roman matron, very white under the black double kerchief of the Iraq head-dress, which tied her brows like a crown. She had let down a piece of her bodice, and a triangle of white skin showed, slowly growing red and angry under the constant limp beat of her podgy, grubby little hand, black-rimmed round the finger-nails. Beside her was a dark slave-type whose African blood shows hysterically under stress of emotion. She had a huge mouth, and thin and waving arms, and her thumbs stuck out and showed the paler inner side of the palms: she did not beat her breast, but thumped hard on the little red notebook where her part was written, with an energy which made one realize how deeply the idea of Vicarious Punishment must be embedded in human nature. Next her stood a very Persian type, close-lipped, with regular features and straight brows; and beyond, a young, cow-like woman,

24

double-chinned, amiable and absent-minded, who had to refer to her notebook at frequent intervals. As they thumped their breasts the congregation thumped with them, and the thick mud walls of the court answered dully to the sound: sometimes the attention slackened; little private conversations sprang up here and there – a special plaintive note from the pulpit was required to get things going again. And presently, after a rest – for the recitation had been going on for an hour or more, and the leaders had changed at intervals – they draped one half of their heads in their black gowns and took black silk veils trailing in their hands: the metre changed from the staccato trochaic to a wailing anapaestic measure: real weeping shook the crowd. In the alcove, behind the arches out of sight, candles were lit; a little procession came in with trays on its head – a tray covered with a green-edged brocade, magenta and silver; four behind it with candles – five or seven on each – pink and white sweets, and a saucer of henna; and a last tray with a jug of water, green lettuce, salt and pepper. As they were borne in, the four leaders reached the ecstasy of their sorrow; they told the story of the death of Husain: they turned to right and left and the sobs of the women followed them as they turned: the women with the trays, weeping too, tilted them and their candles at all angles; until, in a scrimmage, the lights disappeared and the sweets were scattered, every sweet or candle being able to give to its possessor the fulfilment of her wish.

Before the excitement of this climax had subsided we left our places, climbed to our roof, and came away, for curious glances had already been cast towards us. And as we walked back, closely veiled through the dusty street, I thought, not of this violence of passion, but of the august ritual of our own cathedrals, aethereal and remote; and wondered in what similarity of instinct, what selfsame desire to express the inexpressible in visible shape, this too had had its birth. On the last day of the 'Ashura the Persian children in Kuwait are taken to the Mulla, who passes a knife under their chin in sign of sacrifice or dedication; from mythology to religion, from religion to mysticism, the great truths pass: and it is well now and then to see them in those simple forms that belong to our first awakening in this world, so that we may not forget the brotherhood of men. KUWAIT

* * *

Every country has its own way of saying things. The important point is that which lies *behind* people's words, and the art of discovering what this is may be considered as a further step in the learning of languages, of which grammar and syntax are only the beginning. But if we listen to words merely, and give to them our own habitual values, we are bound to go astray.

* * *

The *inscrutability* of the East is, indeed, I believe a myth ... the ordinary inhabitant is incomprehensible merely to people who never trouble to have anything much to do with him.

* * *

It is not *badness*, it is the absence of *goodness*, which, in Art as in Life, is so depressing.

* * *

In a few years' time oil will have come to Kuwait and a jaunty imitation of the West may take the place of its desert refinement. The shadow is there already, no bigger than a man's hand – a modest brass plate on a house on the sea-front with the name of the Anglo-American K.O.C., Kuwait Oil Company. Small camps here and there are pitting the desert with holes, inspired by geology. But the industrial age is not coming here with a rush, as elsewhere: its few representatives are pleasant people who – marooned away from their familiar atmosphere – are learning to deal kindly with a scale of values so different from their own. Their women do not stroll about in shorts and sleeveless among the veiled inhabitants; nor do their men shout abuse at servants unused to the unmannerliness of European speech. Time is everything – and luckily it takes eight months or so to drill an oil hole. . . .*

⬦ ⬦ ⬦

The old order goes. Like the country squire in England, the sheikh is becoming an anachronism: the Latin centralizing conception is ousting the old personal ideas which were common to our Teutonic forefathers and to the beduin of the desert. It is inevitable, as little a matter for complaint as the sequence of the seasons, though one may have one's predilections. But I have often thought that, as far as Britain is concerned, the increase of our difficulties and misunderstandings of late years is largely due to this cause. For we were fundamentally in agreement with the old order: the differences between the feudalism of the East and that of our public schools and Universities was not so great as one might think: and there were many points of contact between a tribal chieftain and the sons of English country gentlemen who ran the Empire. The reign of the Effendi is almost as new to us in Britain as it is in the Orient, and it is small wonder that we now and then have hitches in our dealings with it abroad when we are not yet quite sure as to how we are adapting ourselves to it at home. It is certainly a revolution which has given the *urban* civilizations of the world a remarkable advantage.

⬦ ⬦ ⬦

The police who sit in the three gatehouses might also be dated as you please, Rip Van Winkles from any time except our own. Clad in what to the female mind looks like a voluminous nightdress very much 'off white', amid whose billows the cartridge bandolier must surely get entangled in moments of crisis, the three old men lounge

* From the 1937 edition of *Baghdad Sketches*.

27

on their seat or squat in a windowless den brewing coffee
and keep their eyes on who goes in or out and, in their
toothless way, uphold the rule of law; waiting for the
approaching end of their days with that dignity which is
the keynote of Arabia, made of poverty and leisure, of a
complete unconsciousness of dress as an asset to respect-
ability, or of physical comfort as an essential to happiness.

KUWAIT

⋄   ⋄   ⋄

This is one of the charms of the desert, that removing
as it does nearly all the accessories of life, we see the thin
thread of necessities on which our human existence is
suspended: things which we consider ordinary simply
because they are indispensable, there appear with their
true import made visible: food and fodder and the tem-
perature of the seasons, so near to the terrible extremes
of heat and cold which kill; or simple objects such as
the two flat stones without which corn cannot be ground
and bread made; or the vessels to hold milk or water
without which drinking is impossible (as anyone may
know who has ever stood thirsty by a cow ready to be
milked with nothing to milk her into). What we see in the
desert are a few permanent threads which, overlaid and
hidden by many patterns, run unrecognized through our
more complicated lives and hold them together: so that
living there for a time, we feel that we are re-establishing
the proportion of things in our own eyes, and rediscovering
their values – and water especially we come to hold
precious, seeing, as King David saw, that it is the lives
of men.

⋄   ⋄   ⋄

On the borders of its loneliness, blue-headed thistles
stand like little crucifixes with arms outspread, in endless
rows along the edges of the mounds. The drab disc of sun,
round and small like a moon, scarce shone through the
scudding dust. In the ruins of the great court two jays

flitted with elusive wings, under the dust-coloured colonnade, against the dust-coloured sky, and reminded us that out of this drab material Life itself, so vivid and various, may spring at any time. SAMARRA

❖   ❖   ❖

It is difficult to explain the desert charm, so empty of tangible delights, if it be not the lonely delight of freedom.

> *Libertà ch'è si cara*
> *Come sa chi per lei vita rifiuta.*

You may say that any open space with not a house in view can give that same sense of happy privacy. But it is not true. There is a real significance, a glorious exultation, in the knowledge that behind the horizon, and behind it again, and again and again, for days and days and days, lies the Desert of Arabia. To stand upon the shores of the Atlantic and not know what lay beyond must have been a very different matter from anything open to us at present, when we realize that however far we go, all we shall ever find there is America.

❖   ❖   ❖

But in the morning all is peace, and all went out to pasture. The camels, looking as if they felt that their walk is a religious ceremony, went further afield; they are comparatively independent, needing to drink only once in four days; the sheep and goats stayed nearer. And when they had all gone, and melted invisibly into the desert face, the empty luminous peace again descended, lying round us in light and air and silence for the rest of the day.

❖   ❖   ❖

We sat in a little circle, seven effendis, the Rais Baladiya, and myself, on chairs on the quayside at Kufa, at the northern end of the town. Its one line of houses, small quay, and moored barges with painted blue trelliswork cabins, were foreshortened, and vague in the dusk. Sucking up to the bank with a gurgle now and then, as if to join in the conversation, the Euphrates flowed at our feet, wide in flood. The shaving of a new moon appeared above it, declaring the end of Safar, the second month of mourning; and at the sign of its straw-coloured crescent, a dozen fires or more shone in the palm-tree darkness of the opposite bank: they flickered up and down, waved by the unseen arms, and then drifted for a second or two, burning, down-stream: they are thrown in at the end of the month of lamentation to carry away the sorrows of the year, a custom no doubt as ancient as the river-made land itself. Our modern Iraqis, dressed European, their sidaras on their laps, seeing these flames, glanced up at the crescent *hillal*, and wished each other luck, as unconscious of moon worship as the average churchgoing Englishman when he sings *Halleluiah*.

❖   ❖   ❖

I used to wander of an evening outside the town, under this great wall in the dusk, and admire the new moon hanging above the windowless buttress in a daffodil sky. The women and children of Nejf took the air then and sat about their graves. Their city of the dead drifts out into the desert – no walls are needed there.

❖   ❖   ❖

As I came away the long bazaar was lighted, with busy clusters round the coloured crockery of the eating shops. I walked, feeling in love with all the world, and was sud-denly shocked to see an old shoemaker cross-legged in his booth staring at me with eyes of concentrated hate. One gets these shocks in Nejf, and it is horrid to be hated all for nothing. And what a strange revelation of self-esteem it is when people only love those who think and feel as they do – an extension of themselves, in fact! Even Chris-tianity does not cure us – since one cannot feel right with-out assuming that the rest must be wrong. Personally I would rather feel wrong with everybody else than right all by myself: I like people different, and agree with the man who said that the worst of the human race is the number of duplicates: the old shoemaker was wasting his missionary feelings. And if he had been able to look past my English bodice into my heart, he would have seen that what it was filled with at the moment was a friendly respect for his Shrine, which stands over the souls of men as the golden dome of Nejf stands over the desert, and draws them from afar. I was thinking of the ramshackle khan where old Afghans, having walked across the steppes of Asia, pay one rupee a month for a room to live in the neighbourhood of their Holy Place, ready to be gathered finally into its sacred dust. Their *kilims* for prayer are spread in the courtyard; at the door of each little cell, under a dilapidated wooden colonnade, an earthen jar in a wooden frame drips water-drops from its pointed base into a bowl: and that is all their furniture, more or less. They eke out a living by weaving black wool for tents, staked out on the ground between the *kilims*; and meet once a week for a 'service of remembrance' when, out of their poverty, they scrape each a *fils* (the fiftieth of a shilling) and send it to the Shrine. Who are we to criticize a faith that gives so much?

The Valleys of the Assassins

Persia 1930–2

This is a great moment, when you see, however distant, the goal of your wandering. The thing which has been living in your imagination suddenly becomes a part of the tangible world. It matters not how many ranges, rivers or parching dusty ways may lie between you: it is yours now for ever. So did those old Barbarians feel who first from the Alpine wall looked down upon the Lombard plain, and saw Verona and its towers and the white river bed below them: so did Xenophon and Cortez, and every adventurer and pilgrim, however humble, before them or after: and so did I as I looked over that wide country, intersected by red and black ranges, while the group of hillmen around me, delighted with my delight, pointed out the way to the Rock of Alamut in a pale green cleft made small by distance far below.

❖   ❖   ❖

The mountain shape, first seen as a dream in the distance, alarming as you approach, lost perhaps altogether as you become involved in its outworks and ramifying valleys, appears again suddenly, unexpected as some swift light upon a face beloved to which custom has blunted our eyes. Like a human being, the mountain is a composite creature, only to be known after many a view from many a different point, and repaying this loving study, if it is anything of a mountain at all, by a gradual revelation of personality, an increase of significance: until, having wandered up in its most secret places, you will know it ever after from the plains, though from there it is but one small blue flame among the sister ranges that press their delicate teeth into the evening sky.

❖   ❖   ❖

People who know nothing about these things will tell you that there is no addition of pleasure in having a landscape to yourself. But this is not true. It is a pleasure exclusive, unreasoning, and real: it has some of the quality and some of the intensity of love: it is a secret shared: a communion which an intruder desecrates: and to go to the lonely and majestic places of the world for poor motives, to turn them to cheap advertisement or flashy journalism, jars like a spiritual form of prostitution on your true lover of the hills. The solitary rapture must be disinterested. And often it is stumbled upon unthinkingly by men whose business takes them along remoter ways: who suddenly find enchantment on their path and carry it afterwards through their lives with a secret sense of exile.

❖　❖　❖

What a delicate plant is our civilization, I thought, as I sat in the shade with the circle of the tribesmen around me, in that short silence which is good manners in the East. You would imagine that these people, who know the life of cities and its comforts, would reproduce it in some measure when they return to their own hills. Far from it. They return and live just as they lived two thousand years ago or more. The force of primitive circumstance is too great for them. And these amenities are not, like freedom, or religion, authority or leisure, among the indispensable necessities of mankind.

❖　❖　❖

Out in the sunset the homing flocks poured like honey down the hill-side with their shepherds behind them; beyond the cries and greetings, the barking and noises of the camp, lay the silence of uninhabited mountains, a high and lonely peace.

❖　❖　❖

Solitude, I reflected, is the one deep necessity of the human spirit to which adequate recognition is never given in our codes. It is looked upon as a discipline or a penance, but hardly ever as the indispensable, pleasant ingredient it is to ordinary life; and from this want of recognition come half our domestic troubles. The fear of an unbroken tête-à-tête for the rest of his life should, you would think, prevent any man from getting married. (Women are not so much affected, since they can usually be alone in their houses for most of the day if they wish.) Modern education ignores the need for solitude: hence a decline in religion, in poetry, in all the deeper affections of the spirit: a disease to be *doing* something always, as if one could never sit quietly and let the puppet show unroll itself before one: an inability to lose oneself in mystery and wonder while, like a wave lifting us into new seas, the history of the world develops around us. I was thinking these thoughts when Husein, out of breath and beating the grey mare for all he was worth with the plaited rein, came up behind me, and asked how I could bear to go on alone for over an hour, with everyone anxious behind me.

❖   ❖   ❖

Danger is interesting and necessary to the human spirit, but to do something that will be generally disapproved of, if found out, must be humiliating unless one is so hardened that other people's opinions can have no influence at all. Only a fanatic can be happily a criminal.

❖   ❖   ❖

It is pleasant now and then to go among people who carry their lives lightly, who do not give too much importance to this transitory world, and are not so taken up with the means of living that no thought and time is left over for the enjoyment of life itself.

❖   ❖   ❖

It is a remarkable thing, when one comes to consider it, that indifference should be so generally considered a sign of superiority the world over; dignity or age, it is implied, so fill the mind with matter that other people's indiscriminate affairs glide unperceived off that profound abstraction: that at any rate is the impression given not only by village *mullas*, but by ministers, bishops, dowagers and well-bred people all over the world, and the village of Shahristan was no exception, except that the assembled dignitaries found it more difficult to conceal the strain which a total absence of curiosity entails.

✧   ✧   ✧

We came down into Khava in the sunset when the cliffs of Kuh Garu shine like opals in a light of their own. Mist lay in the hollows and the air was cold. In the village of Beira where we lodged, in the north-eastern part of the plain beside another ancient mound, the tribesmen had not yet moved from their tents into the winter houses, so that we had another evening in the open, roasting pleasantly round a fire of thorn bushes in the middle of the headman's tent, where his carpets were spread in our honour. One side was open: a long line of black oxen with felt rugs on their backs blocked it and acted as a windscreen: they chewed their feed gently through the night, while we slept as well as we could with rivulets of cold air creeping down our spines: now and then some tribesman, pirate-faced in the half-darkness, would rouse himself, heap an armful of thorns on the embers, and fill the tent with strange shadows and a fleeting warmth.   LURISTAN

✧   ✧   ✧

As we rode back, and the valley lay shining before us with the mounds of its cemeteries, or habitations perhaps, plainly visible under the folds of the ground, the great age of the world seemed to be revealed with a sudden poignancy: here men had wandered for thousands of years, their origin and their end unknown. Their dead lie thicker than the living amid these hills.   LURISTAN

✧   ✧   ✧

Zora used to look after me for fourpence a day. With her rags, which hung in strips about her, she had the most beautiful and saddest face I have ever seen. She would sit on the grass by my bedside with her knees drawn up, silent by the hour, looking out with her heavy-lidded eyes to the valley below and the far slopes where the shadows travelled, like some saint whose Eternity is darkened by the remote voice of sorrow in the world.

SHAHRISTAN VALLEY

❖　❖　❖

A worse shock met me as I came down into the court-yard. The sergeant, on his face on a blue rug on the ground, was being bastinadoed: one policeman sat on his ankles and another on his shoulders, and two more were hitting him alternately from either side with leather thongs. The Sardari sat close by on an overturned saddle, and called to me in a friendly way to come up too. The man, he said, had been stealing government cartridges. By this time I had come to the conclusion that he was not really being hurt, though calling lustily on one Imam after the other: perhaps privates are careful how they beat their own sergeants. When the Sardari had counted forty strokes, the two men got off their kicking superior, the executioners folded away their lashes, and the victim him-self rose a little stiffly, but cheerfully, and saluted as if to suggest that bygones should be bygones.　LURISTAN

❖　❖　❖

'Are there any police?' asked *Hajji*, who had been spoilt again by travelling with an escort.

'There were two; they have been shot,' said Keram carelessly, unconscious of the havoc he caused.

He was a charming man. I think he was never afraid, though the country seemed to be thick with relatives of people he had killed, and this was a serious drawback to his usefulness as a guide outside his own tribe. On the other hand, there is a certain advantage in travelling with someone who has a reputation for shooting rather than being shot: as Keram said, in a self-satisfied way, they

39

might kill me, but they would know that, if I was with him, there would be unpleasantness afterwards.

He had a great sense of humour and was excellent at telling a story. He told me how he had been deprived of his gun for shooting the seven pet pigs of the Armenian Governor of Alishtar, the same who had betrayed Mir Ali Khan. The pigs were grazing near the castle, and Keram, like a good Moslem, never imagined that anyone would go to the trouble of keeping such animals; he amused himself by shooting six and laming the seventh. It limped back to the castle just as the Governor came out of the gate for his evening ride. 'What is this?' said the Governor. 'I shot six pigs in the wood,' Keram explained innocently. Whereupon his gun was taken from him, 'and since then,' said he, 'I have had to take to opium; my heart is so sad for the long days in the hills.'

It was the time for his pipe, and I offered to sit by the roadside and wait while he smoked it – a suggestion which evidently touched him, for he repeated it over and over again to his friends as an illustration of the 'Akhlaq-i-shirin' or sweetness of character of women in Europe.

❖   ❖   ❖

The uncle of Amanulla Khan appeared from the next settlement; he looked a villain, but at least a cheerful one; he had a short, thick, red beard, and a roving eye which settled at frequent intervals on my luggage. I had brought very little with me – and nothing in the way of cloaks, bed, field-glasses, or weapons that might tempt a Lur: but even so I always felt there was a certain danger in the few possessions I carried, for there was no mistaking the looks that were cast upon them even among the friendly tribes. My hat was always a great attraction, being made of finer felt than any in Luristan, and I had several times to explain that it was a woman's hat and that men would be ashamed to be seen in it; whereupon it would regretfully be put down.

❖   ❖   ❖

Distant fires of Ittivend camps twinkled in the shadows of the valley and the lower slopes: the cliffs of Peri Kuh rose flooded in moonlight from the darkness: there was an immense and beautiful silence. Just as I was dozing off, *Hajji* crept up, and whispered to me to sleep lightly, for there would be trouble in the night: I opened one eye to watch him creep back and sit, a wakeful and forlorn little figure, guarding his horses in the moonlight: and I heard him no more till, somewhere about the middle of the night, the two men woke me with shouts which frightened away a woman who was creeping from under the back of the tent towards the luggage I was sleeping on.

LURISTAN

❖   ❖   ❖

It is unlucky to reach a nomad's tent in the master's absence.

The laws of hospitality are based on the axiom that a stranger is an enemy until he has entered the sanctuary of somebody's tent: after that, his host is responsible, not only for his safety, but for his general acceptability with the tribe. He is treated at first with suspicion, and gradually with friendliness as he explains himself – very much as if he were trying to enter a county neighbourhood in England, for the undeveloped mind is much the same in Lincolnshire or Luristan. From the very first, however, once he is a guest, he is safe, in every district I have ever been in except the wilder regions of Lakistan.

❖   ❖   ❖

Poor as they were, these people had two guests poorer than themselves, a widow woman and her daughter from Lakistan across the river. 'The widow and the fatherless and the stranger.' Among the nomad one realizes the Bible sorrow of these words; the absolute want of protection, the bitter coldness of charity when obligations of kinship or hospitality have ceased to count. These two women worked about the fields for their small share of the household bread, until they must wander on, weak, helpless, and indifferent to their own fate as driftwood.

❖　❖　❖

'It was a fight,' said he, 'two years ago. I used to live in Harsin then, as I had married a Harsini woman and had a house there. One evening in the *Chaikhana* there was an argument, and I shot someone dead. I was right, but perhaps I did not think before shooting. Anyway, when I had gone home to bed, those accursed Harsinis came round to my house and shouted out that they did not want tribesmen in their town and I was to leave. I got up on to the roof and said I would not leave. They then began to shoot, and I shot back and hit some of them. Then they all surrounded the house, and I went into the upper room which had a small window good for firing from, and we kept at it till the morning and all through that day. The house had high walls so that the people could not get in anywhere; and I had a friend among them outside, and in the dusk he crept up and spoke to me, and I told him to go into the mountain and call the tribe. Meanwhile the Harsinis knew that I always smoked my pipe of opium in the evening, and counted on getting into the house when I had to stop firing. But my wife was a good woman: I put her at the window with the gun, and she continued to shoot while I smoked, and hit a man, she says. Anyway, we kept it up all that night as well, and next morning just at dawn, *tik tak*, we heard shots all around in the hills, and we knew that the Kakavends were coming. Our tribe numbered 8,000 fighting men then before these last year's wars. Well, the Harsinis also knew that the tribe was coming down upon them, and they scattered like rabbits. My wife saddled my horse, and I rode out alone to meet the tribe, and came back with them up here into the hills. And I have never been into Harsin since.'

'And what did you do with your wife?' said I. 'I hope

you took her with you. She seems to have been a useful sort of person.'

'I sent for her afterwards,' said Keram. 'I have her still,' he added, as if it were a rather remarkable fact. 'I am fond of her. She is as good as a man.'

⟡   ⟡   ⟡

The dust-storm raged all through that night.

Tired out with the sound of talking, of which the day seemed to have been more full than usual, I left the Zardushtis early and took refuge in a mud-walled cubicle both from the tribesmen, who sat on their carpets outside in the moonlight, and from their women, of whom only two or three ventured from their own part of the tent to watch my evening toilet. When I had undressed and washed, and had tried, to their rather fearful delight, the effect of cold cream on the faces of two gay young brides, I was left in solitude and darkness, while the dust swished in showers through the dry leaves of the roof above my head. The slight mud wall, here in the waste of open spaces, turned into the very emblem of solidity; no comfortable safety of London houses, with shuttered curtained windows and draught-proof doors, has ever seemed to me so sheltering as those six feet of upright earth buffeted by the Arabian wind.   PUSHT-I-KUH

⟡   ⟡   ◆

Shah Riza is really a maker of quilts, but he looks like a philosopher, which, in his way, he is. His philosophy is one of passive resistance to the slings and arrows of fortune as they hurtle round him: he sits among them looking as if he thought of something else, but ready, in his quiet way, to make the most of any lull in the general perversity of things. As an attendant he left much to be desired – everything in fact if an attendant is supposed, as I take it, to attend. But he was a charming old man, and would sit for hours, while all was bustle around him, filling little tubes of paper with native tobacco, lost in what one might

43

take to be the ultimate perfection of resignation, but which was really a happy daydream, far from the toilsome world in which I was looking for keys or dinner, or any of the other things he was supposed to see to.

❖   ❖   ❖

Thieves were around after dates, which hung in moonlit clusters on the palm trees, and Mahmud would wake at the slightest noise and go prowling round. But as a matter of fact there was little enough chance of sleep for anyone, for the moon went into eclipse, and a beating of tins from every roof, a wailing of women and frenzy of dogs, and occasional high yelp of jackal made chaos of the night. I sat up at last and tried to explain the solar system to Shah Riza, who was smoking meditatively, squatting on his hams.

'They say,' said I noncommittally, as befitted so unlikely a theory, 'that it is the shadow of our world which hides the moon."

Even the Philosopher's mild abstraction was roused.

'That,' said he, 'is quite impossible. Anyone can see from here that it is an insect which eats the moon. It is alive. It has a spirit. It means war and trouble coming. But it is only a sign, and Allah will not allow it to go too far.'

As if in answer to his words, the moon, a red and sullen ember, began to reappear: the blackness of sky dissolved again slowly into luminous spaces: the rattle of tins subsided: and, leaving the matter of the solar system unsettled, we were able to sleep.   PUSHT-I-KUH

❖   ❖   ❖

The handsomest people in Baghdad are the Lurs of Pusht-i-Kuh. They stride about among the sallow-faced city Shi'as in sturdy nakedness, a sash round the waist keeping their rags together, a thick felt padded affair on their backs to carry loads, and their native felt cap surrounded by a wisp of turban. They crouch in groups

44

against a sunny wall in winter, or sleep in the shade of the pavement, careless of the traffic around them, and speaking their own language among themselves: and you will think them the veriest beggars, until some day you happen to see them shaved and washed and in their holiday clothes, and hear that they belong to this tribe or that tribe in the mountainous region that touches Iraq's eastern border, and find that they are as proud, and have as much influence in their own lonely districts as any member of a county family in his.

❖ ❖ ❖

It is only the unexpected that ever makes a customs officer think.

❖ ❖ ❖

The valley was now full of loveliness. A last faint sense of daylight lingered in its lower reaches, beyond the village houses whose flat roofs, interspersed with trees, climb one above the other up the slope. Behind the great mountain at our back the moon was rising, not visible yet, but flooding the sky with gentle waves of light ever increasing, far, far above our heads. Here was more than beauty. We were remote, as in a place closed by high barriers from the world. No map had yet printed its name for the eyes of strangers. A sense of quiet life, unchanging, centuries old and forgotten, held our pilgrim souls in its peace.   SHAHRISTAN

❖ ❖ ❖

The dawn crept dove-coloured over the solitary landscape, subduing the high ridge before us to a uniform shadowy gentleness; even as the mind of men, growing in wisdom, may yet subdue and smooth away by very excess of light the obstacles before it.

❖ ❖ ❖

The Mirza was an ascetic – one of those sad-faced Persians with tired eyes and gentle manners, pathetically

45

thin, who spend their lives meditating inaccurately on abstruse subjects, and are roused to mild enthusiasm over beautiful and harmless things like calligraphy.

They knew about Hasan-i-Sabbah: they thought it natural that one should journey from England to see his castle. The Persian's mind, like his illuminated manuscripts, does not deal in perspective: two thousand years, if he happens to know anything about them, are as exciting as the day before yesterday; and the country is full of obscure worshippers of leaders and prophets whom the rest of the world has long ago forgotten.

    ◇   ◇   ◇

The Persian love for the ornaments of life pierces through religion in the domes of Shah Abbas: mistily lost in their blue patterns they melt above our heads like flights of birds into an atmosphere part heaven and part the pale Iranian spring. The seasons of this world are ever remembered: in the Masjid-i-Shah, the 'Royal Mosque', at the bottom of the oldest polo ground that is now the open space of Isfahan, the four liwans (the covered spaces) are built for the four seasons, one by an artist from Kerman, the other three by Isfahanis; the differences of their carpets are visible in the pattern of their domes, and the temper of meditation rises from its sectarian hedges into the air of peace. Walking there under the building of the craftsman, 'the humble one, the Servant of God, the Isfahani, who requires your prayers', one thinks of mosques and tombs scattered over Asia, fragments of a splintered turquoise sky that covers the Muslim world.*

    ◇   ◇   ◇

The great religious leaders have all come from Asia: it is the more spiritual continent, we are fond of saying. But perhaps it is also because the woes of mankind are here so much more evident; the need for reliance on

* From 'The Golden Domes of Iraq and Iran', *Cornhill Magazine*, Spring 1961.

something more universal than human charity is so much greater; and the deep and tender hearts of the prophets are more inevitably awakened by the sight of human suffering. The Ages of Darkness produced saints: perhaps their relative scarcity at the present day is the result of a higher standard in ordinary comfort and kindness.

❖   ❖   ❖

There were three charming women. I left the men outside and came to them by the fire out of the night wind. An older woman with a sweet and gay face, was mistress of the tent; it was her daughter, and a daughter-in-law, and a friend, who had brought us in, and showed us off as a delightful find picked up by rare good fortune. I soon discovered that I carried a kind of radiance about me, a magic not my own, derived from the city of Baghdad from where I came. The two young women had spent a few months there when their husbands worked as coolies, and the memory lived with them in a glorified vision. They stroked my clothes with a wistfulness pathetic to see.

'Kahraba,' electricity! I lit my torch and they murmured the word as if it held a whole heartful of longings. The worship of the East for mechanical things seems to us deplorable and shallow; but seen here against so naked a background, the glamour of the machine, of something that gives comfort without effort in a place where bare necessities themselves are precarious, and every moment of ease comes as a boon and a miracle; seen here by the fire in the tent that swayed in the cold night, the light that sprang at will from the palm of my hand did indeed hold a divinity about it – a Promethean quality as of lightning snatched from heaven and made gentle and submissive to the uses of man. So their eyes saw it, more truly, perhaps, than ours, who buy the thing as soulless glass and wire.

❖   ❖   ❖

The tomatoes were cooking in a pot while our hunger in the meanwhile was being stayed with raw cucumbers.

47

Our meal was evidently looked on in the nature of a banquet. Every now and then the mother of the family gave it a stir, tasted it, and nodded with an appreciation beyond mere powers of speech. Four little boys, subdued with expectation, sat in a silent row, while a smaller infant amused himself with two lambs, tied up in the tent near the fire out of the way of wolves, and evidently used to being treated as members of the family. The little daughter, the prettiest woman's eldest child, busied herself with household jobs, knowing well that her chance of the feast was remote.

And presently the dinner was cooked: the tomatoes were poured out steaming: they had dwindled, alas, and now only just looked presentable on three small pewter plates, one for me, one for the Philosopher, and one for the two muleteers. Such as they were, they were put before us, while the family looked on in admirable silence: only one boy, unable as yet quite to control his feelings, followed the plates with his eyes; his tears rose slowly, the corners of his little mouth turned down. His mother, ashamed, gave him a small slap and then, surreptiously, offered him her fingers to lick, on which some savour of tomato still lingered.

I myself was hungry enough to have demolished all three dishes at once with the greatest ease; but who could withstand so heart-rending a spectacle? To say anything was impossible: our hostess would have been humiliated beyond words: but one could leave part of the dinner on one's plate. I pretended to be satisfied half-way through the microscopic meal, and the four little boys lapped up what remained. As for the daughter, she had learnt already what is what in this world. She neither got nor expected a share.

❖ ❖ ❖

Two weddings were now in progress. The bride from Pichiban was expected at any moment. She had a three hours' ride down the precipitous track from Salambar to negotiate under her *chadur*. She was coming: a beating of wooden sticks and drums announced her; '*Chub chini ham Iaria. Chub chini ham Iaria*,' the boys cried, dancing round her. A vague and helpless look of discomfort made itself felt from under the *chadur* which hid the lady on her mule, all except her elastic-sided boots. Two uncles, one on each side, kept her steady on the extremely bumpy path. So, in complete blindness, the modest female is expected to venture into matrimony. The village seethed around, waiting. The lady approached, riding her mule like a galleon in a labouring sea. At a few yards from the door she was lifted down: a lighted candle was put into either hand: in front of her on trays they carried her mirror, her Qurán and corn and coloured rice in little saucers, with lighted candles: these were all borne into her new home, but she herself paused on the threshold with her two lights held up in white cotton-gloved hands; and her bridegroom from the roof above took small coins and corn and coloured rice, and flung it all over her as she stood. The little boys of Garmrud were on the look out: a great scrum ensued for the pennies: the bride, unable to see what was going on and with the responsibility of the candles, which must not blow out, in her hands, swayed about, pushed hither and thither, and only sustained by the buttressing uncles: it is as well to have relatives at such moments.

With a great heave the threshold was transcended: in the shelter of her new home the lady unveiled, while the bridegroom, paying her not the slightest attention now he had got her, devoted himself to our reception.

GARMRUD

❖   ❖   ❖

Love, like broken porcelain, should be wept over and buried, for nothing but a miracle will resuscitate it: but who in this world has not for some wild moments thought to recall the irrecoverable with words?

Traveller's Prelude

Autobiography 1893–1927

When I was twelve years old, my grandmother died, and all the cocoon of furniture and ritual which swathed her showed for the lifeless thing it was and vanished. We were in Italy at that time, and the news came to the Tuscan sea-coast, and I took it with me and sat with it in the sun-warmed shadow of a wooden jetty, where carts drawn by many pairs of oxen brought the white blocks of marble from Carrara to load in tethered coasting vessels with furled yellow sails at the end of the pier. The sun lay like a cape of state, heavy and white, on everything around. The sea shone beneath it, a burning mirror with darkness in its depth. The sand was fragments, like everything in this world: bits of mother of pearl, shining mica, marble, white, green or black, could be recognized among the tiny particles that made it, and here and there a fluted shell lay dull and opaque, undigested by Time.

In the middle of this dazzling emptiness the fact of death first stood before me, the strange cessation of something that has been and is no more. 'Never, never, never, never, never!' The house so intimately remembered, the rustling slow descent of the stairs every day in the middle of the morning; the face, like a pale Rembrandt above its ruff of black lace, with skin soft and loose; these things belonged to the only permanence we had ever known – and they had ended as a road might end with a wall built across it, and no clue to the further way. I sat a long time, I remember, not thinking, but contemplating the collapse; no one explained these things to us at that time; I sat till the thought of food made me run home – barefoot into the cool house with its tiled floors, where milk and dishes of grapes and figs buried in leaves awaited us at tea-time; and death was forgotten, though the first wrinkle on the face of the world remained.

❖   ❖   ❖

Very few people can dispense with the trappings of their lives and yet feel themselves secure; and these are remembered as victors, though they may be crossing-sweepers by occupation: they are seen independently of the furniture of their time.

❖   ❖   ❖

Perhaps the best function of parenthood is to teach the young creature to love with *safety*, so that it may be able to venture unafraid when later emotion comes; the thwarting of the instinct to love is the root of all sorrow and not sex only but divinity itself is insulted when it is repressed.

❖   ❖   ❖

All the feeling which my father could not put into words was in his hand – any dog, child or horse would recognize the kindness of it.

❖   ❖   ❖

She had a genius for forgetting her own mistakes as well as other people's, which is in its way a form of generosity.

❖   ❖   ❖

Half the marriages that go wrong are destroyed by too much amiability at the outset; each human being has things that in the long run he cannot assimilate or forgo – and to try to do so only means a slow accumulation of disaster. It is far better to know the limits of one's resistance at once and put up as it were a little friendly fence around the private ground.

❖   ❖   ❖

The unexpectedness of life, waiting round every corner, catches even wise women unawares. To avoid corners altogether is, after all, to refuse to live.

❖   ❖   ❖

54

A good many men still like to think of their wives as they do of their religion, neglected but always there.

❖ ❖ ❖

A plurality of affections is not so bad, if there is enough to go round.

❖ ❖ ❖

When one is in love, there is no shadow of doubt or hesitation: but when the imagination alone is engaged, and begins to meet the solid substance of reality, an invincible reluctance comes, in spite of oneself. If a man is impetuous enough, he can probably overcome it and make a happy marriage, but not, I feel sure, the happiest: that absolute willingness which comes so rarely to a woman is a feeling which nothing else can replace . . .

❖ ❖ ❖

Everyone develops his own soul in the world, and the crime of crimes is to interfere with this process in those you are responsible for; perhaps that is what is meant by Christ's word about children.

❖ ❖ ❖

The garden was our universe. It stretched downhill in a solitude peopled with birds, frogs and tadpoles, and hedgehogs in the twilight, which we carried home in a ball and waited to feed with milk when they unrolled. The place had once been an orchard and was filled with fruit trees of every sort; and its gentle life busy with tiny incidents in the sun and dew – its loneliness – with only an old gardener, usually out of sight, and my father among the daffodils – and the careless abundance – circles of fruit on the ground beneath their boughs – gave it an atmosphere which I have never met again except in the descriptions of Eden in *Paradise Lost*.

I first noticed how the sound of water is like the talk of human voices, and would sometimes wake in the night and listen, thinking that a crowd of people were coming

55

through the woods. All really good sounds are composite –
even the song of birds which is helped and varied by the
air it floats in; and the noise of crowds, and voices of
wind, with sobs and lighter squeaks and whispers in it;
the single human being's speech, made out of all his
ancestors and all his past; and the sounds of water, moorland streams and alpine brooks, the waves on sand or
shingle, or the drone of the water wheels of Hama.

❖   ❖   ❖

The whole coast, on summer nights, was full of vitality
and business. The boats with their lights at sea, the stars
almost tangled among them, the fishermen wading with
lanterns after octopus among the seaweed and rocks, the
fireflies that, with a luminous mist, filled the Aurelian
way, all made a sort of orchestra so that you could not
tell where land or sea or sky began. In boats near the
coast, carrying a headlight, fishermen speared the illuminated water; the half-naked figures, lit from below,
looked like moving bronzes as they flung their spears.

❖   ❖   ❖

At five in the evening one came out into darkness – dim-
lighted buses like glow-worms, and searchlights and moonlight tangled and lovely over Trafalgar Square. The
Strand was crowded with Colonial troops most anxious
for company, and when I had a cold I discovered that
any slight cough would bring two or three huge Australians
looming out of the night like the hulls of ships, so that I
had to hurry along, desperately sucking lozenges.

❖   ❖   ❖

The centre and gain of all my life at college was W. P.
Ker. Since the age of fifteen, when I met him privately at
Viva's, I had recognized his silent quality. I liked him so
much that Viva asked him again: he became my adopted
godfather, and I used to go to his lectures for the pleasure
of it. He taught me all I know in English literature and

56

corrected one of my essays by writing underneath it: 'Too many words.' He used very few himself, but always careful and good ones. He would come late to his class, with a pile of books in his hand, his head a little forward as if it were stretching over a chasm, his pince-nez dangling by their black cord in one hand. He would tiptoe down the theatre at University College with the same step he used on a mountain path, looking neither to left nor right, while a gentle stamping of students' feet showed him how popular he was. He told me that he disapproved of more than three-quarters of an hour for any lecture and came late on purpose. No one missed if he could avoid it. He would say what he wanted in the shortest way and then open his books and read out of the authors themselves the things he wished you to remember. Many pieces live with his voice in my memory, but most of all the bit about the Oxus in *Sohrab and Rustum* and some bits of Dante which he would quote and suddenly look up at me, after we had climbed in Italy in the hills. He never insulted his classes by under-estimating them: you could pick your treasures out from his three-quarters of an hour: but if you missed them it was your own affair – he never underlined them, and you had to do your thinking for yourself.

❖   ❖   ❖

For the first time in my life I climbed with a rope; and it was W.P. Ker who taught me: the happiness was almost frightening, for it seemed more than one human being could manage. The rope was only for six minutes or so at the top of the ascent of a small excrescence called Le Petit Pousset – but the feeling was there, the extraordinary sensation of safety, the abyss held in check, the valley with its life of everyday, bridges, tracks, fields and houses, seen from a narrow ledge which made it exciting and remote; this sense of *double life* is, I think, one of the main ingredients of the mountain sorcery.

❖   ❖   ❖

I was the first 'lady' who came to work in a hospital in Bologna. The nurses were *all* women of the streets; only one was respectable, having been seduced by a doctor and stuck to him until he left her: she was called Norina, and was capable, pretty and embittered. The others carried on their two professions at once and it was so well-known, the doctors told me, that their evidence was never taken in a court of law. I had a strange and uncomfortable feeling with them long before I knew this: only Norina I liked. They hated me at sight, and were horrid out of jealousy: until at last I went up to them and asked what it was all about, and explained my feelings about the war (which, of course, had not yet touched Italy) and what it meant to us all, and they were kind to me ever after. I was sorry for one or two who looked sad and wistful; one especially who used to stop the others from making jokes when I was there, because – I once heard her say – 'she isn't like *us*.' Since knowing them, I have never felt that there is a real barrier between different sorts of women, only differences of the accidental sort that divide all human beings.

❖ ❖ ◆

The air service was still very young. They dressed me in sheepskins and (as it was hard to move at all, so wrapped up) lifted me across some part of the engine to the little double seat in front with all open except for a wind-screen before it. The observer sat down beside me, but there was never a thought of strapping in: when I noticed that the rush of the engine had lifted me on to my feet, and that the observer beside me was holding on to the screen in a determined way, I did so too. I have never enjoyed an air journey so much. The observer shouted out names of towns below, but they were blown away before they reached me: one could put one's head out from the screen a second, and feel as it were the rush of the world through space. When we reached Le Bourget, there was no place reserved to change in, and I was apparently expected to drive into Paris in my dishevelled state: I explained to the customs official that this was impossible: a mirror must be found. 'It is only reasonable,' said the French Customs. A mirror *was* found, and placed on the bench among the luggage – and I am probably the originator of the first thought for female comfort that ever crossed the mind of an air-line. Very soon afterwards, a lunatic shot the pilot of a London–Paris aeroplane from my little front seat, and it was forbidden to passengers.

❖   ❖   ❖

. . . . Asolo, a tiny but complete city forty miles from Venice, laid out in the lap of a hill under the shell of a cruiser-shaped pre-Roman fortress. Below it is a little square with trees, and a fountain that spouts from under the pedestal of a fat lion sitting on its haunches; on a low spur opposite is the castle tower of Catherine Cornaro, last queen of Cyprus, who kept a gay provincial court here when Venice had bought her from her island. It is a sleepy little town, well away from railways and main roads. Its streets are lined with crooked porticos, irregular and at uneven heights above the road, each house having decided for itself the shape and altitude of arches it liked best; and most are whitewashed, though a few painted façades remain with dim but splendid colours. Two ragged walls descending from the fort cut off a segment of steep green hill and then embrace the town; they have now mostly been built into houses. Our own home is beside an archway in this wall and its library is built on the thick and solid foundations of the guard-house.

❖   ❖   ❖

. . . The garden was quite small, but it had all a garden needs, a pleached alley of hornbeams over-arching, a statue of Bacchus under dark laurel boughs, and masses of iris that seemed to focus the colours of the plain and of the far Euganean hills. The wall of the house was heavily clustered with a rose called Fortune's Yellow, and the memory of its rich bunches, nectarine-coloured in a blue spring sky, comes to me as a symbol of happiness even now.

❖   ❖   ❖

Many feet have walked our Asolo garden since its small Roman arena first was built to please a country audience; I have often thought of them in long-shafted afternoons, when light lies like the garment of the centuries upon the plain below. Dearer figures have now joined that quiet procession, moving about the paths in a familiar air that has a clearness, a more essential reality than life. I shall not forget them, though I shall be forgotten before long; so fluid are all earthly shapes. Who can pass through Europe in these years and not constantly think upon this? But goodness has in itself such royalty that when we see we recognize it as immune from death: we think of the lives that embody it as heart-beats of a Timeless radiance, small temporal pulses of Love itself, and therefore everlasting.*

* Extract from the Preface to her mother's account of Asolo and a fascist prison in 1940: *An Italian Diary* by Flora Stark (published three years after her death by John Murray, 1945).

Beyond Euphrates

Autobiography 1927–37

... difference is between the wild and the tame ... I have come to the conclusion that one of the main differences is that of habitually making or not making up one's mind. Every wild animal lives in a state of danger, which means deciding all the time, while the very essence of tameness is the absence of any need for decision. The wild soul is perhaps conscious – as I certainly am always conscious – of the intrinsic danger of life, which is hidden from the domesticated, whether animal or human, by the fact that their necessities are provided for them, and only a strong imagination or accident can make them realize the precarious nature of what they rely on.

... it does not do to assume the domestic alone to be laudable in a world where all the chances of survival are with wildness. On the other hand it would be unfair to assume that wildness alone is brave: there is a slow and steady noble courage needed to face, sustain and conquer domestic life. The wild are perhaps the more fearless as opposed to courageous; their minds more mobile and their instincts more ready, by necessity, to face the unexpected when it comes; and whether they are beduin, untamed birds and beasts, or eccentrics like ourselves, mere captivity is likely to kill them.

❖   ❖   ❖

I am willing to risk my life, not from any natural fearlessness or recklessness. I am careful of the things that I need to enjoy life: careful of money, health as far as may be, and time as far as I can: these are necessary. But to be careful of life itself is to assume that it is more important than what is beyond life. To risk one's life seems to me the only way in which one can attain to a real (as distinct from a merely theoretic) sense of immortality unless one happens to be among the lucky people in whom faith is born perfect.

❖   ❖   ❖

It is wise to discover what our happiness is made of. Of the ingredients of which mine is made I think the presence of goodness comes first, and the affection of a few people I can understand and care about is second. The third is sunshine. After these, and close upon them, comes some sort of daily beauty, preferably a spacious view; and after that and side by side – expressions perhaps of the same desire – domestic servants of an old-fashioned friendly sort, and an atmosphere of sequence in time, a regular procession and not a disorderly scramble towards eternity. I like to have as much as possible of the background of this procession in sight, and could never live happily for long in a country where no winding footpaths have been made by the steps of my predecessors. That is why I care little for deserts, unless a caravan route, crossing them, makes the long human endeavour, the slow repeated victory, more plainly visible by the nearness and constant obvious possibility of defeat. United to this feeling for time as it passes, so that I will not even separate it, is a delight in learning as much of the world as I can before I leave it. I think that these pleasures – all receptive – are more essential to me than my own work. They mean more than any applause or esteem, for the voice of other people only touches if it carries affection; and I can imagine nothing more barren than to be admired and not loved.

❖ ❖ ❖

The wealth and variety of love can be counted upon to overflow all loss: the general richness will compensate those who cross hither and thither on our path, while we make straight for the targets of our heart.

❖ ❖ ❖

The magic of art is that it inspires inanimate objects with some of the qualities of *life*, so that they can create pleasure, and satisfy obscure needs for colour, or rhythm, or form: the art of dress perhaps brings these qualities into the closest relationship with ourselves; and a woman who has no use for it must have some secret obliquity, arrogance or malady of soul. I suspect anyone self-satisfied enough to refuse lawful pleasures: we are not sufficiently rich in our separate resources to reject the graces of the universe when offered; it is bad manners, like refusing to eat when invited to dinner; and indeed I should call humility in religion the equivalent of good manners in ordinary life.

❖   ❖   ❖

I hate philanthropy and am averse to teaching, in a world where the pleasant occupation is to learn.

❖   ❖   ❖

I am naturally disposed to take the unexpected easily, and therefore belong to that half of the human race whose enjoyment of life seems to annoy the other half. It is one of the things I have found most disconcerting and most unreasonable in my life.

❖   ❖   ❖

There is little leisure to discover what lies around us, and so much – presumably – for what is beyond; and it has long seemed to me to be the behaviour of a rather ill-mannered guest on this planet, to wolf his earlier courses and ask for port and coffee straightaway.

❖   ❖   ❖

I dislike being an anvil for the hammering out of other people's virtues.

❖   ❖   ❖

So small a Universe, at fifteen, and so much of it outside oneself. In spite of all that is said, it is happier later where the joy and the value of learning about it all is discovered, and our self comes to count for so little that its unhappiness scarcely troubles one. The ageing body need not impede the spirit very much. But never for a moment, if one desires this true contentment, can one

65

think in terms of this life only: the proportion with eternity must be kept.

❖   ❖   ❖

Conventions are like coins, an easy way of dealing with the commerce of relations.

❖   ❖   ❖

Most people, after accomplishing something, use it over and over again like a gramophone record till it cracks, forgetting that the past is just the stuff with which to make more future.

❖   ❖   ❖

Did I tell you of the Dronero priest's sermon against football? He says it is anti-Christian because it concentrates everybody's attention on people's legs.

❖   ❖   ❖

From the open windows of my mother's little factory, the click of the shuttles and the thread of her five silk-looms came like the voices of pigeons in the East, harsh but blurred, monotonous as water, and now and then, like a break of wave above it, a snatch of song.

❖   ❖   ❖

I dislike the sea anyway when it is anything more than something blue that wraps itself round islands. Yet as I lay in my bunk between distasteful meals I read the *Odyssey* for the first time in Butcher and Lang's translation; and the roar and hiss of the waves was a part of its music. I was so transported with delight that I leapt up at intervals to walk about the narrow cabin floor, in an ecstasy that had to be expressed somehow, or choke me. Except Shakespeare, who grew from childhood as a part of myself, nearly every classic has come with this same shock of almost intolerable enthusiasm: Virgil, Sophocles, Aeschylus and Dante, Chaucer and Milton and

Goethe, Leopardi and Racine, Plato and Pascal and St. Augustine, they have appeared, widely scattered through the years, every one like a 'rock in a thirsty land', that makes the world look different in its shadow.

❖   ❖   ❖

A new venture mixed with the known ingredients of one's life makes a sort of patina like that of bronze or marble, or the lustre of ancient glass, an iridescence created by one layer of time on another, where both shine through.

❖   ❖   ❖

After four days we came to the Rockies; cold green rivers carried slabs of ice in the sun; russet larches appeared among the firs; and my father stood on Creston platform to meet me, looking old as I had never seen him, his face more wrinkled than the bark of an elm, his clothes creased, folded and fallen into a sort of permanence of age, his movements difficult – and only his blue eyes shining in this ruin with a tranquil clear transparency, gay if it had not been so quiet. He lifted the end of his stick slightly, from far away . . .

The cottage gave him one of the few essentials of his life – a view; and I made a small place for myself opposite, and spent most of the next four winter months there, in a quiet companionship that shone like a miniature, very small and bright, in a great melancholy frame. . .

To me, in the long winter evenings, Time itself seemed to burn like a still candle without a wind, consuming the waxen minutes imperceptibly; and only now and then, a gust from the outer world, the thought of the best years wasted, the operation still to be faced, the precious East attained only to be lost, and the impossibility of writing or studying in the little window-seat when interrupted even by the best of talk, came like a crisis of frustration and made the huge country round me, the immense separation of prairie, forest, lake and Atlantic beyond,

seem like those fabled landscapes by the Styx, an un-
bridgeable waste of desolation, fit only to be peopled by
the dead. These thoughts came in the night, or when I
was alone; the sight of my father's old face, where – among
all the wrinkles – the years had never been able to trace
a line that was not noble, filled me with tenderness – and
thankfulness too that I had reached him: one's good angel
has such hard work to make one do the right things, that
I have a feeling of gratitude independent of myself when
he succeeds.

✧　✧　✧

. . . my father spoke of my future travels, and took perhaps
more pleasure in the thought of them than in most things:
and who shall assess the part of our joy that is taken up
with dreams? Those who can distribute this happiness
are not to be despised, though their own share of merit
may be small enough.

✧　✧　✧

I thought I had never seen the grip of winter so cruelly
shown, draining the light out of water and forcing it to
flow below, voiceless and dangerous, blind under a slip-
pery security, and separated from the living air.

CANADA

✧　✧　✧

The Mirza says it is well to rise early, for the hour between dawn and sunrise is taken from Paradise.

✧　✧　✧

I think I would go on my knees to true *excellence*: but
why go into ecstacies over the moderate virtues merely
because they might not have been there at all?

✧　✧　✧

Music at the Temple, clear as falling water, thin and
rare and fine: not luxuriant as the music of Santa Maria

68

Maggiore. The eighty-eighth Psalm, filled with grandeur and terror and awe. As they sing, the great barren land lies before me, so pitiless, so utterly without refuge. In spite of all, our generations in Europe are too comfortable to produce literature like this.

❖ ❖ ❖

The Anglo-Saxon seems to have a talent for religion and none for saintliness.

❖ ❖ ❖

It is well to be familiar with the contemplation of death. We follow him, as he carries our friends away, until the strength of the world bids us turn back and live; the shadows then sink into the dark more gently than seemed possible at first.

❖ ❖ ❖

The Puritan attitude which grudges happiness belongs only to those who have never entered very deeply into life.

❖ ❖ ❖

Sometimes all our centuries, from the Neolithic days, the first chippings of flint, the monolithic temples, the rumours of Phoenicians, Greece and Rome, the first rude mason's chisel on Gothic saint, the wool merchants and men in small boats on coasting ventures, the excitement of learning, policy and politeness and the new subtleties of faith and the hiss of steam – all gather together to press within us to our Present, like the strength of a rower gathering to his stroke: and to us who live so much away from England, perhaps these moments come with a particular intimacy, reminding us of that to which we belong.

❖ ❖ ❖

Nothing is more useful to a woman traveller than a genuine interest in clothes: it is a key to unlock the hearts of women of all ages and races. The same feeling of intimacy is awakened, whether with Druse or Moslem or Canadian. I wonder if men have any such universal interest to fall back upon?

❖   ❖   ❖

The women sit out with their tents open on the sunny or shady side according to the time of day, and show us their old barbaric jewels and magic beads. The daughters of the Jinn were once bathing when some wolves rushed out and frightened them and they all turned themselves into stones: and there they still are, and the beduin find them – often old cornelians and agates or Assyrian seals from the mounds that are scattered like green islands over the buried cities all around us: and they wear them in strings at their belt with a silver thing with bells or tassels to dangle at the end, and have a meaning for every stone; some bring children, or cure serpent bites, or, if they touch a man's cloak, will make him instantly love you: and one, which was offered to me as a present yesterday, is to be rolled on the carpet and any woman you happen to dislike is brushed out of existence on the instant: this is called the 'carpet stone'.   IRAQ

❖   ❖   ❖

The unexpectedness of the Arab is that he does not allow himself to be much influenced by the bribes he takes.

❖   ❖   ❖

No medium has yet been devised for the translation of life into language, nor can any words recall the dazzling fluidity of days. Single yet fixed in sequence, they fall like the shaft of a cataract into time and through it.

❖   ❖   ❖

There are some countries in which, at every visit, one recaptures the magic of a first arrival: Greece, Italy and Persia are such to me. However often, misted with sand, I leave the hot borders of Iraq and climb the Paitak pass and, through the cliff-gate of Sar-i-Pul, come on to plains where the larks sing over nests hidden in flowers; and see slow clear rivers under bridges bent like bows; the tumbled mountains of Kermenshah and poppy fields of Kangevar; the Asadabad pass and its grassy shoulders where the sun seems to lay a separate mantle of gold on top of the green; and the high gentle wave of Elvand south from Hamadan – however often I may see them, I think there will always be that tightening at the heart which comes with the remoteness of beauty, just beyond the possible footsteps of men.

❖   ❖   ❖

I am not often disposed to regret what happens, whether my own doing or that of others, and feel life rich on almost any path; it is a lean employment of time to brood on what might have happened along some other turning. But I do regret the time wasted on unrequited affection. It is like a duet solo, or those silly bouts at tennis for exercise, with no one to send back the ball: there must be something that can at least be imagined to be alive at the receiving end. The natural heart loves as it beats, and the sooner it can turn from a sterile expense the better: and for this reason I regret walking so long down a one-way lane with only a blank wall at its end.

❖   ❖   ❖

Pictorial art has to express tangible objects, not ideas, and the very fact of its being lower in degree than philosophy also means that it can be perfect without superior aid: just as we prefer an 'artistic' and not a 'philosophical' cook.

❖   ❖   ❖

I do think that the average Englishman is naturally antagonistic to ideas as such: he sniffs and sniffs at them like a pony at a bog, while everyone else has long been getting to the other side.

❖   ❖   ❖

71

The Qurán has been their one source of inspiration for centuries: it is their background – and however European-ized they may be, one is sure to get nearer to them *really* if one comes at them from behind as it were, through the things they knew as children, or that their parents and nurses knew, than if one comes through the medium of a new civilization which means something quite different to them from what it means to us. When I take the old Mulla's standpoint, I know where I am and what to expect: when I take a European standpoint with a 'civilized' oriental, I can never know where I am, for I have no means of judging what 'European' means to him: it is certainly not what it means to us.　HAMADAN

❖　❖　❖

A lot of observation lies under common figures of speech. One's heart stands still, or sinks, or leaps; one sees red, or is frozen with horror: no more accurate words could be found to describe what actually these feelings are. And it is ever our figurative thinking that is *accurate*, gives, that is to say, the unmistakable picture of what we intend. When they carry a picture, the simplest words can hold an extraordinary weight of meaning. Who for instance but one accustomed to the desert horizon could say like the Psalmist that the Lord has removed our sins from us 'as far as the East from the West'. When we think of the words, we see what the Psalmist saw, and it is the fact of his having seen it that makes it live – not a deliberate skill with words which can never take the place of real vision.

❖　❖　❖

The only way to be hardened to uncomfortable con-ditions is not to know of a comfortable one.

❖　❖　❖

On this Persian journey I first stood consciously on the edge of death. This I think is rarely done if you are attended by others in a sick-room, where it is their business and not yours to estimate your chances. But, alone and in the open, the trench where the world ends is very near, as if it were a part of the unexplored landscape around you, with love and fear and the days of your life in its dark. Later, I have been afraid, but this time all seemed a part of the far valley and its austerity, and I was subdued to a sort of timeless peace. I have thought of this since when travelling in the Western Desert and watching the twisted metal that marks the places of so many dead, and have been comforted by the hope that those, in their lonely ends, were visited by the same final gentleness, remote from men and their fatiguing ways. The thread that held my will to life in those days was the thought of my father: I must not die before him, I thought again and again, hoping to spare him a useless grief. And when I reached Teheran I found a letter, telling me of his death during those hours when I lay ill in the hills.

❖   ❖   ❖

Though human loves come second on the list, coupled with the sun, I have also had, ever since childhood and no doubt in my very bones, a curiosity due to detachment. It is not really detachment but rather a *wideness* that makes me feel intimately about a number of things that to many people are remote and strange. Every view, to appeal to me, must have a distance; every friendship, a depth below the surface; every work of art, some quality brought out from the unknown.

❖   ❖   ❖

I have come to the conclusion that to put off doing troublesome things is really a much more serious fault than it looks; I think it means a lack of will-power, for you will notice that *no* nation which has this defect will ever get on: it means that it hasn't got the backbone to make itself do something it doesn't like, and of course there is no hope for it.

❖   ❖   ❖

Yesterday I saw an amazing sight. The testing of a drill hole for oil. It meant burning a lot of waste oil as it poured from two pipes at the rate of 50,000 barrels per day. The flame rushed out in two jets roaring like tumbling stones in a mountain torrent. One felt the great heat about 300 yards off, and the actual fire must have risen to about 150 to 200 feet, pouring out in yellow masses with dark rolls of smoke on one side, which then stretched away right over the sky. The yellow fire was soft and frothy as new milk, or the snow of an avalanche, and covered with these rolls of smoke like transparent leafless woods on a hill-side: now and then a black shadow thrown on the brightness made a strong contrast; the two jets showed against the fiery mass by darker shadow and blue light playing round them. Dark light shone on the lake of oil on the ground over which the fire swept. It looked wonderful in the middle of the peaceful empty landscape, throwing its long shadow over the shallow hills. People were ploughing, taking their teams of horses to the nearest possible point so that the fire rose like a curtain behind them: they said the heat in the ground would ruin their melons. All this waste of fuel was to rest the pressure from the oil well.

❖   ❖   ❖

One of the pleasantest of all days was spent in the desert train. It travelled once a week from Amman to Ma'an. Turkish slit trenches still showed round stations where T. E. Lawrence had hovered with his sticks of gelignite. But there was now no feeling either of drama or hurry: the wide white sky, the pale earth like an embroidered tent below it, no trees, but here and there a ruin, or fort, or well: outlines of camels, and riders with their striped cloaks in the sun; and, when the train, puffing its smoke like a leisurely pipe, came to a standstill, the song of larks above it clear and high: all these things built their harmony in the desert elixir of air; and the train, washed through and through with light, surrounded by emptiness, seemed to lose that feeling of congestion which we associate with the mechanic age. I think one may become fond of machines, as one becomes fond of people, if there is space enough around each one to see it clearly, so that its individual dignity remains. A plough is beautiful on a hill-side of furrows, or a car alone on the loops of its road; and there is all the difference between crowds and processions, merely because in the latter every creature has a place and space to move in. The same may be said of most vehicles, and of a fleet at sea. The feeling for space, which is respect for the individuality of objects, is an invention of humanity unknown to nature, who crowds all things regardless of individual perfection: and that is why I like open landscapes best, or else an arranged view – a park or tidy cultivated slopes – where the struggle is either invisible to us, or has actually been done away with by the selectiveness of men.   JORDAN

The Southern Gates of Arabia

1934-5

The Ambassador from next door came staggering along against the wind, his shawls and turban billowing in circles round an equally circular face, cheerful and placid and decorated with a gold tooth; a twitter of female conversation had been rising from his cabin and he explained that it was a widowed aunt returning to Mukalla. I called on her, and found a woman singularly beautiful for an aunt, swathed in thin veils of flowered chiffon, crouched on the narrow sofa which she evidently found much less comfortable than an Arabian floor. She had the type of face one comes to know in Hadhramaut, very long and narrow, with a mouth large but sensitive and easily smiling, and brown eyes, brilliant, large and dark: a long neck and a necklace of gold beads. She welcomed my presence as that of a sister in this wild and unpleasant world of waters, whose effects she was trying to mitigate with buttery pastry; she felt the need, she said, of something heavy inside to keep things from going round and round. The pastry I felt sure would soon be going round too with the force of an animated tombstone, and I left before the catastrophe, after inducing her to risk decorum by opening an inch of porthole. In the clean, buffeting openness of outer air, I walked about reflecting on this extraordinary female ideal of travel in shut boxes through the world, to see and be seen by as little of it as possible.

❖   ❖   ❖

I have often wondered why a ship appears to be on the whole a more satisfactory possession than a woman. It is probably because, being so frail an object, precariously and visibly balanced between the elements, even the most obtuse of men realize the necessity of attention and tact at the helm. But women, though quite as fragile, perched on edges more razor-like, though intangible, amid eternities even more momentous, must evidently give a false impression of stability, since belated and absent-minded

79

jerks so often take the place of that gentle hand upon the tiller which keeps both ships and human beings along their course. Hence the natural but unreasonable preference of peace-loving men for ships.

❖   ❖   ❖

The water was green as paint below; little wooden huris ran in and out with round oars; I sat in a shallow boat between my new protectors, carefully shaded under the black umbrella, with a delightful feeling of being at home and happy in all this clamour: while the Captain, leaning over his bulwarks, his face a picture of distress and pity, said to me: 'God keep you safely,' in a voice eloquent with forebodings which would have surprised no one so much as the friendly and hospitable crowd of 'wild men' whose brown bodies, shouting and bending over their oars, were landing me on the steps of Arabia.   MUKALLA

❖   ❖   ❖

This was the great frankincense road whose faint remembrance still gives to South Arabia the name of Happy: whose existence prepared and made possible the later exploits of Islam. On its stream of padding feet the riches of Asia travelled: along its slow continuous thread the Arabian empires rose and fell – Minoan, Sabæan, Katabanian, Hadhramaut and Himyar. One after another they grew rich on their strip of the great highway; their policy was urged by the desire to control more of it, to control especially the incense regions of the south and the outlets to the sea: they became imperial and aristocratic, builders of tall cities; they colonized Somaliland and Ethiopia and made themselves masters of the African as well as the Arabian forests.

❖   ❖   ❖

... the wide sand foreground of the estuary, whose sober

80

colours gather themselves discreetly to a climax in the living browns and fawns of camels couched in circles.

⋄ ⋄ ⋄

There is not much to be bought in Mukalla, and most of it is food of some sort set out in open baskets and made invisible by flies. There is no local manufacture except that of the curved daggers and of baskets large and vividly dyed. The drying of fish, of sea-slugs (*Holothuria edulis*) and of sharks' fins for China, the dyeing with indigo, and pressing of sesame oil, comprise the industry of the town: the Indian Ocean is a good highway, and most things come by sea; and the little business there is centres round the harbour, where dhows show their riggings and high sterns against the background of cliff, and black slaves with huge naked limbs lie asleep on the bales of the custom house, waiting for a load.

⋄ ⋄ ⋄

Here in sheds dim with aromatic dust and impalpable spicy perfume, where pale bars of sunlight lie on the half-transparent gums, women bend their veiled heads over the shallow baskets, and with small hennaed fingers sort out the various grades [of frankincense]: while the sailing fleets, making for home, load up their antique holds with drums of petrol.   ADEN

⋄ ⋄ ⋄

As we drove back by the sea, along the strip of wet sand at the edge of the waves, gulls rose like a fluttering grey ribbon before us and sank again behind. They live here in countless numbers. They seem black and white as rain-drops when they fly against the water. On the white sands they look like white pearls, and like grey pearls on the brown, and they swim strung out like pearls upon the waves. Now, as their barrage rose and fell, they made a canopy of shadow with their wings. They rose only just high enough to clear us, wheeling and almost touching; and one misjudged his distance and hit me and fell stunned in my lap. I picked him up, stiff with fear; only his eyes moved, surrounded by a delicate black beading like the glass of a miniature; his beak was red, its upper point curved over the lower; his feet were webbed and pale; and as I let his body slip away to freedom, the grey feathers felt cool and smooth as the sea they live on.

❖   ❖   ❖

When the evening came, and the sweet shrill cry of the kites, that fills the daylight, stopped, 'Awiz appeared with three paraffin lanterns, which he dotted about the floor in various places, and, having given me my supper, departed to his home. The compound with its dim walls, its squares of moist earth planted with vegetables and few trees, grew infinite and lovely under the silence of the moon. The gate of the city was closed now; a dim glow showed where the sentries beguiled their watch with a hookah in the guard house; at more or less hourly intervals they struck a gong suspended between poles, and so proclaimed the hour. And when I felt tired, I would withdraw from my veranda, collect and blow out the superfluous lanterns, and retire to my room. None of the doors shut easily, so I did not bother to lock them; I had refused the offer of a guard to sleep at my threshold, the precaution was so obviously unnecessary. As I closed my eyes in this security and silence, I thought of the Arabian coasts stretching on either hand – three hundred miles to Aden; how many hundred to Muscat in the other direction? the Indian Ocean in front of me, the inland deserts behind: within these titanic barriers I was the only European at that moment. A dim little feeling came curling up through my sleepy senses; I wondered for a second what it might be before I recognized it: it was Happiness, pure and immaterial; independent of affections and emotions, the aetherial essence of happiness, a delight so rare and so impersonal that it seems scarcely terrestrial when it comes.

MUKALLA

❖   ❖   ❖

Quiet and friendly, his word was final, and I wondered what the gift of authority is, that makes one man's words mean so much more than those of another: an inner definiteness, perhaps, the courage to face and accept responsibility and therefore to come to decisions in one's own self? It is a quality which even animals understand and obey.

❖   ❖   ❖

One man particularly I remember. After squatting on the sand beside his camels to wash his arms and legs and head and mouth, he stood to pray. One could not see in the late light that he had anything on at all (though in the middle of the prayer he did as a matter of fact loosen and hitch up his futah). He stood there with a pose graceful and sure, his beard and hair and lean unpampered limbs outlined against the sand and sea – just a man, with an indescribable dignity of mere Manhood about him. And when he had stooped to place his forehead on the ground, he came upright again with one spring of his body, as if it were made of steel.   MUKALLA

❖   ❖   ❖

Here are the oil presses, about twelve open sheds built for shade, where a blindfolded camel – a little basket covering each eye – walks slowly in circles for ten hours every day and pulls a pole weighted with boulders, by which the upper millstone grinds the seed. The seed is in a sort of funnel in the centre, which holds about 36 lb. and is filled five times a day. The camel carries on his dreary circular task with his usual slow and pompous step and head poised superciliously, as if it were a ritual affair above the comprehension of the vulgar; and no doubt he comforts himself for the dullness of life by a sense of virtue, like many other formalists beside him.

MUKALLA

❖   ❖   ❖

The camel is an ugly animal, but, like some plain women, has lovely eyes, brown and soft with long lashes – often the only gentle things to look at in its sun-hardened world: but this one beauty is little noticed, for – though the adored is often compared to a gazelle – who has ever heard anyone say of her that she has eyes like a camel?

❖ ❖ ❖

There is a cheerful quality in the neat brisk sound of trotting donkey feet on hard ground. And it is pleasant too, to sit on a donkey pack, when you know how to do it, without rigidity, meeting the jolts and caprices of your companion with an elastic temper and a capacity for balance, riding, in fact, as one rides through life, with a calm eye for accidents and a taste for enjoyment in the meantime.

◆ ❖ ❖

Out in the wadi a caravan from San'a in Yemen was trailing in, with small donkeys gambolling unloaded about the hulking camels. The men were tall, unlike our beduin of the jōl, bearded and aquiline, and friendly. They came they said vaguely, from the direction of prayer, 'qibli,' as they call the north-west beyond which Mekka lies: they cracked their fingers towards its sun-hidden spaces, while their caravan, a hundred camels or so, laden with sacks of millet, waited and lifted their slow heads and blinked in the sun.

❖ ❖ ❖

The routine of our journey had begun, unexpected in its small incidents, immutable in its unchanging lines: this interplay of accident and law, the surprises of every day worked into a constant pattern by physical necessities compelling people along the same paths for one century after the other – this surely is the charm of travel in the open: and when our human methods of transport are so perfect that physical laws no longer regulate our journeys by land or sea or air, why, then we shall have outgrown our planet: and that delightful feeling of oneness with its animals and plants and stones, oneness in the grip of the same compulsion, will have gone from our wanderings for ever.

✧　　✧　　✧

All our doings were part of a ritual which many centuries have gone to elaborate, and which alone makes it possible for the beduin to travel in harmony through the hardships of their lives. They treat each other with a tacit formal courtesy, made second nature by custom; and I never saw any of them shirk a piece of work when it came, or wait for another to get up and do it after the heavy day. When one thinks how difficult it is for two friends to live together in tolerable comfort; how travel books are strewn with such remarks as 'Here so and so and I parted,' leaving much to the imagination – this good-humoured courtesy of the beduin, always on the extreme edge of discomfort or hunger, deserves to be remarked. Travellers who go among them with servants of their own are apt to find them quarrelsome, rapacious and difficult; but nearly all those who have been alone with them have a different tale to tell. One is then accepted into a rough but cordial brotherhood; its duties are made light and its comforts are enlarged for the weaker stranger: one sits in the best place available after a comparatively easy day, through which you have ridden and they have walked, and watches them in their cheerful labour; and realizes how the society of the wilderness has its social disciplines and restraints, its rules of decent living, just like any other society of men.

HADHRAMAUT

✧　　✧　　✧

I woke at 3 a.m. and looked for a long time into the dome of the sky, limpid as a well of light. Some bird, perhaps an owl, whistled from the shadows: a great hard

85

brilliance shone on our world of stones. The wind still rushed through the motionless tree whose leaves were too small and hard to bend before it: it showed its swift feet in white clouds from the north that billowed up glittering to be swallowed and melted in moonlight. The frozen air shimmered, the moon rode high, but the opposite western sky was soft under an avenue of stars. Orion and Gemini there led a friendly train, far from the white abyss which steeps the moon in loneliness; like a procession, unutterably lovely, they moved over the uninhabited lands, beautiful to themselves alone in their nightly wandering. No wonder the ancient peoples of Arabia worshipped these heavenly beings: they seemed almost to touch the barren surface of the jōl in their passing: here, so near the Equator, they seemed to step more swiftly over the enormous girth of the world. Presently a great bank of cloud came and overwhelmed them; and drizzled upon us till the dawn.

HADHRAMAUT

✦ ✦ ✦

In this clear altitude, where the basic forces of the earth are building, it seems absurd to reckon time in human years. The scrubby plants are scarce more momentary than men who pass in transitory generations, leaving no more trace than does a fly on the steady hand of a craftsman at his labour. Our origins and histories become almost invisible against the slow lifting of the jōl. Only the beduin, who have little to lose or fear, walk over it with an unburdened spirit, naked and careless, 'butterflies under the arch of Titus,' and know its scanty pastures, and love its inhuman freedom.

✧ ✧ ✧

The oasis below was shut in the wadi bed like a picture in a frame; beyond it – a larger frame – lay silence. How few of us in Europe know silence in the night: even if we sleep alone in Alpine pastures we are comforted by the sound of running streams. But here, between one village and the next, there is nothing except the wind when it blows: and on a still night, that waterless silence is so still that you may fancy you hear in its arid quiet the growth of the desert scrub beneath its breastwork of thorns.   THILE, HADHRAMAUT

❖   ❖   ❖

The wadi is about a thousand yards wide and drops a thousand feet or so with sheer walls. On the rubble sides which hold the cliffs, little towns are clustered, built of earth like swallows' nests, so that only the sunlight shows them against the earth behind. Five or six are visible on the slopes as one looks down. Between them and their squared ploughed fields on either side of a white stream bed, the wadi bottom is filled with palms. Their tops glitter there darkly, like a snake or a river, with scales or ripples shining in the sun. The eye, sated with open spaces, rests on their enclosed greenness, and follows it to where it winds from shadow into sunlight between the buttresses that hold it in and turn it round a corner in the distance. The River of Palms, shut in the adamantine walls, held as it were in a crack of the jōl, looks as valiant and prolific, as optimistic, as full of quiet resting-places and of shadows, as life itself in the arms of eternity.   DO'AN

❖   ❖   ❖

From my window I could see Shibam and its five hundred houses clustered like one fortress above a filigree of palms. On the dusty space in the foreground, camels were treading out the corn. They dragged a palm log in a circle round and round: the men, as they gathered up the straw in sheaves, sang a song together.

Everything in the Hadhramaut is done with singing. The houses are built with songs from the first mixing of mud and straw for their bricks to the last touch of whitewash to their cornice. Even the camel has its special song; the bedu croons it gently as he bobs to and fro: the camel pads along and turns its head contentedly from side to side; and the two together make such a picture of domestic happiness as they jog through the sunlit solitudes of their lives, that I have often wondered how many married couples understand each other as intimately as they do.

❖   ❖   ❖

Seiun is the most delightful of towns. I never got tired of driving leisurely through its scattered ways of houses white and brown. From their slanting walls and upper lattices they look on dusty streets unpaved and silent, and solitary save for a woman here and there trailing her long blue gown by some carved doorway, or beduin camels that brush the roughened mud-built corners with their loads. The houses are rich with every variety of delicate lace-work: from the warm shadows below, their parapets rise into sunlight, often with outcrops like the machicolations round old castles where hot oil was poured on assailants, but here made with the more peaceful object of letting the harim look down invisible on what goes on below. The harim often, too, has a humble little front door of its own, beside the big one. There are many quiet sunny lanes, with a white mosque, or an ornate siqaya, and a palm or two to shade it: and the drains in Seiun are all covered, and run into covered cisterns of mud made smooth and shiny outside, so that one can wander about with no thought of sanitation, in perfect peace. It is, indeed a clean and pleasant town, with a mosque built in the old fashion with seven rows of columns, a market, the Sultan's castle, and the cemetery all in the centre, as in a feudal town it should be: and on market days the white mass of the palace rises between its four corner towers out of a sea of camels, a crowd of sellers of goats and sheep and donkeys, weavers of baskets, squatters over vegetables on the ground, weighers out of salt, dried fish, peppers, and odds and ends of nails and cords and sandals, and women in tall hats selling shawls.

❖   ❖   ❖

In the West, spasmodically and with uncertain hands, we try now to eliminate the *causes* of sorrow: but it is only recently, and since the decline of formal religion. The East still holds religion in its established forms: and encourages philanthropy, which deals with effects and not with causes. For as soon as you investigate and try to alter the origins of things, you are no longer a philanthropist, but a revolutionary, and your disinterested movements are liable to make whole edifices crumble: and mankind is asked from successive pulpits to leave the fundamental things alone. So the East accepts slavery, mitigating its effects with kindness, and thinks no more of this bodily servitude than we do of the slavery of the mind, chained to the daily written words of more capricious masters.

❖   ❖   ❖

We insult and corrupt people by treating their goodness as if it could be paid for, and think the worse of them when they use us merely as creatures who pay. For there is nothing more subtly insulting than to refuse to be under an obligation.

❖   ❖   ❖

What is wrong with the human race, that, having bought at so high a price the fruit of the tree of knowledge, it cannot even use it to tell what it likes from what it doesn't? Not ignorance, but laziness and cowardice prevent us from knowing what we like. Left to themselves, the untaught make lovely things, but when we begin to think that we *ought* to admire or despise, we think the thoughts of other people, too indolent or too fearful to discover our own: and the dear old Sayyid, who loves his carved doors when he looks at them, and finds happiness in his ancient town – the only city I have ever seen whose dignity and beauty no jarring note distracts – considers himself bound to bring our Western ugliness to spoil it for ever.

❖   ❖   ❖

The babies were the playthings of the harim, and suffered, I thought, from overwrought nerves due to the constant avalanche of caresses to which they were subjected as they were handed from one lady to the other among the coffee cups. The older children ran in and out and brought the latest news from one house to the next. They came freely into my room, and so did anybody else – slaves and mistresses, beduin girls round-faced and healthier than the towns-women, and old men and women in need of medicines. A friendly democracy accepted all: the grubbiest could sit there on the carpet, using it as a handkerchief, or lifting the edge now and then to spit carefully underneath. It was the life of the medieval castle in all its details; a life so much lived in common that privacy and cleanliness are almost unobtainable luxuries. Saintliness, on the other hand, is made not only possible, but frequently essential.   DO'AN

❖   ❖   ❖

It was a dense female parterre, glittering and gorgeous, ringed by a black slave crowd. The dresses were brocade or tinsel, stiff with embroidered silver breastplates and necklaces in rows; and heavy anklets, bracelets and girdles, and five or six ear-rings in each ear. The ladies came in with a yellow kerchief tied over their head, but this was soon taken off, and then they showed the elaborate works of art – their face and hands and hair. They wore about a hundred tiny plaits tight to the head from a smooth straight parting painted orange with henna; on their forehead the hair was plastered to a point shining with grease; their chins were bright yellow; the palms of their hands reddish brown with heavily scented henna and oil and painted outside in a brown lacework pattern, like a mitten. Their eyebrows were painted brown and a curling brown pattern darted from each temple; a brown line ran down the forehead and chin. Some were very pretty, with pointed faces and long small chins; but they were in-human, hieratic and sacrificial; not women, but a terrifying, uncompromising embodiment of Woman, primeval and unchanging. And more so when they stood up to dance, one or two at a time. They did not move their feet, but threw their heads and upper bodies stiffly about, and made patterns like wheels in the air with their pigtails. A clinging scent came from their bodies; the drums beat; the bracelets and girdles jingled; the heat was almost unbearable. When one arose, it was like a flower, some many-coloured tulip, opening as she slipped from her dark street wrapping and stood to let her finery be seen, nonchalant but not without an ear for the murmur of discriminating praise. The bride was, of course, invisible in an upper room. More guests kept on arriving: space was made for them, impossible as it seemed: the drum went on beating with its subtle excitement of monotony; more and more dancers stood up knee deep in the female sea: and I slipped out as quietly as I could, oppressed with a mystery so ancient and fundamental, so far more tenacious in its dim, universal roots than the transitory efforts of that incurably educational creature, Man. MUKALLA

❖ ❖ ❖

In the evening coolness, with half a bar of sunset cloud pushed like a sword from behind the rim of cliff, for the whole sunset is not visible from Seiun, I called on the Abu Bekr ladies: they were listening to the 'Music of 'Urfa', which we had left stranded in the river-bed: the four female musicians with their drums sat cross-legged in a row against the wall, one young and two middle-aged and one old: they had rough and hardened faces, for it is not a reputable profession and they are little thought of. One of the medieval kings in Yemen is said to have poisoned himself when, his city having been taken by the enemy, he saw his concubines forced by the victors to dance and sing in public on the wall.

The music was wild, with a low falling cadence, like a waterfall: the women sang in parts, taking on the story from one to the other, beating on the three little drums with an occasional bang on the biggest: I listened hypnotized, as one listens to the breaking of waves.

✧   ✧   ✧

Zarathustra perhaps found in his words the secret of the wilderness. For it allows us to look for a while on our universe from a detachment of loneliness; to weigh our values at leisure; to judge them anew in the presence of things almost eternal. Some we reject, and some we make our own: whatever the result of our weighing, ignoble it cannot be, thus born under the majestic visible eye of Time; we come back with a firmer step into the general world of men.

✧   ✧   ✧

I was losing my strength. I could not see my watch, but listened to a tiny pulse in my ear like a wave of life breaking on some unmapped shore, and waited for it to cease: when it did so, I should no longer be there to know: the thought was terrifying and strange, as every new venture must be. It was not my sins that I regretted at that time; but rather the many things undone – even those indiscretions which one might have committed and had not. I was not troubled with repentance or sorrow, but rather, in a quiet light, saw the map of my life as it lay, and the beauty of its small forgotten moments: tea on an English lawn in summer, gentians in the hills, hot sweet scents of pinewoods in the south – all small and intimate things whose sweetness belongs to this world. I tried to think of them, for I knew that I must keep my mind as cool and quiet as I could. Salim lifted my head at intervals to feed me, with as much tenderness as any nurse; he was a perfect servant, devoted and understanding. He had a charming ugly face, long with a narrow chin, and the big sensitive mouth common in the Hadhramaut, and a high forehead which the white skull-cap, tilted back to the very verge of his shaved head, caused to appear even higher. He looked at me with infinite compassion and moved quietly.

92

Towards morning I slept for three hours, and woke from happy dreams; I had been with my father in some Mediterranean city, luminous in the opal sea; my friend came laughing towards me in a firelit room; I woke with these companionships still upon me and saw the sun on the spiky palm leaves light against the window. There was a twittering of birds; a pleasant air came from the garden and dangled the crochet mats on our small tables; it was the earliest, charming hour after dawn. For a second I forgot that I was ill; and then realized that this was indeed my last day, unless Mahmud the chemist arrived from Tarim with some new medicine. My own methods had failed one by one; the heart was now so faint that I could feel no pulse. The whole affair seemed unreasonable, monstrous, and inevitable, with the world around me and my own mind so pleasantly alive; so it must seem on their appointed day to men condemned to die.   SHIBAM

✧ ✧ ✧

Virgil is one of the most restful of the classics to be ill with. No other poet that I know has so many or such lovely images of sleep, of the quiet of night and the resting earth. And I found, too, something greatly inspiriting in his disinterested, pagan fortitude of death.

✧ ✧ ✧

Psychologists tell us that the impulse of sex is the fundamental mover of this world, and we are perhaps getting a little tired of hearing it so often. But there are two impulses stronger than desire, deeper than love of man or woman, and independent of it – the human hunger for truth and liberty. For these two, greater sacrifices are made than for love of person; against them nothing can prevail, since love and life itself have proved themselves light in the balance; and the creature man is ever ready to refute the Matter-of-fact Realist and his statistics by

93

sacrificing all he has for some abstract idea of wisdom or freedom, unprofitable in every mercenary scale.

❖   ❖   ❖

The love of learning is, indeed, a pleasant and universal bond, since it deals with what one *is* and not with what one *has*.

The Coast of Incense

South Arabia 1934–8

It is usually a chord and not a note that we remember.

♦   ♦   ♦

But here ... comes the main difficulty of writing, the disentangling in its transient cocoon of what is enduring. For how is one to know, among details of which none is too small to have its eternity somewhere, where the apparent greatness may dissolve on feet of clay. On the sure discrimination, the writer's immortality depends.

♦   ♦   ♦

Geologists may see their years in terms of time; musicians in some echo that dies in air; the poet strains language beyond the bounds of telling; the physicist sees diagrams of force rather than forms; the historian watches himself as one wave among waves of sea; but to us, who delight in maps, the idea of life inclines to be spatial – we see it moving from point to point, like a road if we are disposed to attribute its shaping to men, like a river, if we have more feeling for the unexpectedness of nature.

♦   ♦   ♦

The general rule of women is the jungle rule, only to be mitigated, and that imperfectly, by advancing years, hopeless plainness, or the total elimination of men.

♦   ♦   ♦

The portion we see of human beings is very small: their forms and faces, voices and words, their ages and race perhaps: beyond these, like an immense dark continent of which their obvious self is but a jutting headland, lies all that has made them – generations vanishing into the barbarous night; accidents and impacts not only on themselves but upon their forebears; the cry of the conqueror, the sighing of slaves. Even the chemical variation of substances – airs, foods and waters – are all gathered to that

97

point of light which is the person we know. He himself is unable to communicate, forced to use fluid words as if they were solid, and – if Anglo-Saxon and well brought up – is anyway not expected to wish to communicate at all. And when two human beings meet even in the most simple intercourse, it is not the tiny visible substances, but the immense invisibles that come together. It is these that must determine the liking and disliking over which we have so little control.

❖ ❖ ❖

One is apt to think of people's affection as a fixed quantity, instead of a sort of moving sea with tide always going out or coming in but still fundamentally *there*.

❖ ❖ ❖

From love one can only escape at the price of life itself; and no lessening of sorrow is worth exile from that stream of all things human and divine.

❖ ❖ ❖

Absence is one of the most useful ingredients of family life, and to dose it rightly is an art like any other.

❖ ❖ ❖

That supreme goodness which carries unimpaired into old age the capacity to love.

❖ ❖ ❖

Perhaps the secret of a happy life is the feeling of an aim in one's journey, so that one may take pleasure in the milestones as they pass. And this of course is the triumph of religion, placing its goal safely beyond the frontier of death.

❖ ❖ ❖

It is more and more borne in upon me how wrong people are to judge events from the time of their accomplishment and not from the moment of their *thought*: the real action is when one *thinks* a thing – the rest just an unrolling of consequences. It is inevitably frightening to see the consequences come rolling in so irreparably after the thought which had started them is already so far past: people try to deal with actions, which are merely consequences and cannot therefore be any longer vitally affected: and leave the actual causes of events lying unnoticed and untended around them all the time.

❖   ❖   ❖

The methods of power are barbaric, and civilization becomes corrupted as it seeks for power: direction, advice, service are its road, and along that unobtrusive highway it will meet with nothing but reverence and welcome. The recognition of this limitation is the secret of the long success of churches and – when they forget it – the explanation of their fall; and in the chain of Arab countries from Tunis to the Levant one can see European failure becoming sharper in the measure in which this basic secret is forgotten.

❖   ❖   ❖

A great deal is said and written about the struggle between Asia and Europe, and nowhere can it be seen in sharper relief than along the south Mediterranean shore: but I think the problem has nothing to do with continents or races, but is simply a question whether civilization has or has not the right to exploit: if the voice of Christianity is any voice at all, it stands for the equality of human souls, and the fascist revival of the catchwords of pagan Rome was both futile and impious. The good work of the Italian régime was invisible to me at that time; the saddest point was apparent – the madness of absolute power plunging into unnecessary war. And the heartless anachronism, if it had succeeded, would have been accepted by the world.

❖   ❖   ❖

It seems to me that the only thing for a pacifist to do is to find a *substitute* for war: mountains and seafaring are the only ones I know. But it must be something sufficiently serious not to be a game and sufficiently dangerous to exercise those virtues which otherwise get no chance. There must be something *heroic* in life, and no amount of enthusiasm over material things like good drainage and infant welfare, etc., will give this heroic life to more than a very few people. In fact there *must* be danger. The problem is to find a sufficiently dangerous alternative for war, and then half the jingoism of the world would vanish.

❖   ❖   ❖

What happens in tragedy is the coming to life of our background. It has always been there quiescent, a vast, amorphous, unanswered question into whose shadow we never venture very far, but take its immobility for granted. Because we have grown up with it, we forget it; the spot-light is on the little foreground of ourselves. And suddenly those vast outlines are shifting: the vagueness that we had taken for solid landscape is moving down upon us; great rocks and obelisks are crushing out ruin and death. Whether private or public, this seems to me the essence of tragedy – the sudden irruption of the background of life into the small, well-ordered, tender and fragile garden of men.

❖   ❖   ❖

The history of the Middle or even of the Dark Ages will never again be mere history to me, since I have lived in it and known what it has been. Its difference from our world went far deeper than outward circumstances: it went beyond its permanent insecurity, which is now no longer a stranger in Europe: it was perhaps the *acceptance* of insecurity as the foundation of life. This gave to every-thing, even to very small things, a significance, a sharper outline as it were, such as you may find in Gothic carving or Elizabethan writing: the whole landscape is illuminated by an eternal light. People have told me that this has happened to them in concentration camps and has given a serenity even to terrible horror. It is, I feel sure, the secret of great art in difficult ages, and the truth of the commonplace that the artist must be unhappy to be great. In the Hadhramaut a permanent threat to human existence was taken for granted: under its hard light the important and the unimportant disentangled themselves, and goodness and courage remained: and any number of figures that might pass unobserved among the milder outlines of what we call civilization, stand there with a strange majesty and grandeur, as clearly remembered as companions in war.

⬦　⬦　⬦

Sakkara was far lovelier, and we descended into a tomb and saw its walls covered with delicate and most beautiful reliefs, some painted but the most pleasing, to my mind, not. All the dinners the man was to eat through Eternity were being brought to him, chiefly bread and goose: it was an awful thought that so long a series of menus was in the hands of your heirs and survivors. . . .

⬦　⬦　⬦

It always surprises me to notice how short a time is taken by events that have been so slow in coming. In war, in love, in history, in art, and in everybody's life, the long preparation, conscious or unconscious, rushes to its climax and is gone. The cleverness of living is to distribute climaxes – to savour them beforehand and to remember them after in such a way that the labour of their making is lightened and the memory of their passing is without regret: for one might as well take to drink as seek for climaxes all the time.

⬦　⬦　⬦

The abstract world is surely one of the essentials for living in the East: it gives an oasis always at hand wherever one may be.

101

A Winter in Arabia

1937–8

All day we ploughed along the Arabian coast, watching the changing colour of the sea. From the morning's sapphire to the afternoon, shot silk like a kingfisher's wing and barred with luminous shafts, it grew white in the sunset, its underlying darkness showing only in smooth and oily shadows. The tossing flecks of foam in mid-ocean, like tritons suddenly diving, all subsided. The detail of the coast grew clear of haze, the west a stair of gold. Inland ranges with sharpening tops showed thin as paper above their misty flanks. The seagulls' crescent wings against the west were unfathomably dark. The ocean, too, darkened like old black cloth gone green with age.

In the morning at seven we wakened off Mukalla, grey and dove-like in the dawn, to a sea alive with fishing porpoises: their sharp perpendicular fins make the small sudden splashes of foam. Gulls flying low above their heads were fishing too; and so were the men in huris, paddling their round oars. Man here is happy; he joins in the activities of his universe: he lives in a pleasant companionship with the porpoises and gulls. The sailor in his ship is happy too among the gulfs and islands of his round world, whose weathers and vicissitudes he shares; his inventions have not outstripped his mind. But we are now companionless in a universe in which we are unique; our pressing need is to find some harmony which once more may include us with forces equal to our own, greater than those our science has outrun.

❖   ❖   ❖

Between rows of breakers the shallow wave water shone pink and brilliant as its cold smooth shells. Amethyst mountain ranges ran out to their wild capes. Grey cranes with ragged wings rose in slow flight above the tossing water. On the shore some black quick-moving figure of bedu stirred among the rushes like an incarnation of the night. And once, as we came back in the dusk, four small humped cows impeded us: they wandered unattended to the water's edge, dipped their noses in the breaking waves, and appeared to be drinking the sea.   MUKALLA

❖   ❖   ❖

It is, I believe, a fallacy to think of travellers' qualities as physical. If I had to write a decalogue for journeys, eight out of the ten virtues should be moral, and I should put first of all a temper as serene at the end as at the beginning of the day. Then would come the capacity to accept values and to judge by standards other than our own. The rapid judgement of character; and a love of nature which must include human nature also. The power to dissociate oneself from one's own bodily sensations. A knowledge of the local history and language. A leisurely and uncensorious mind. A tolerable constitution and the capacity to eat and sleep at any moment. And lastly, and especially here, a ready quickness in repartee.

❖   ❖   ❖

I cannot help wondering *why* we should so often look upon health as a creation of our own, considering that we accept beauty as a gift from heaven: the same hand presumably fashioned our inner and outer tissues.

❖   ❖   ❖

The tall houses were all lit up: a whispering and a gaiety goes on behind their high illuminated lattices through the sleepless nights of Ramadhan. As in a well the medieval streets lie silent in the stench of their open gutters; no tread wakes the echo in their dust. A moan of prayer came from the lighted mosque as we passed it; camels and donkeys were couching in the square; a soldier sat at the gate, wide open in the moonlight. It is kept open late in Ramadhan.   SHIBAM

❖   ❖   ❖

The fast of Ramadhan is over, and the feast has begun. The gun went off after dark last night, and the new moon must have been visible at least an hour before, but its appearance has to be verified and confirmed by various elders. Sometimes it has been seen on three different days in the towns of Tarim, Shibam, and Hureidha, and the day of the feast has varied in each. The Archæologist, when I told her that the date was not yet certain at sunset last evening, looked cold disbelief; there is no denying it, the Hadhramaut calendar is quite unscientific. But who cares about that? The very steps of the servants are rejoicing through the house. Everyone has blossomed with lanterns or songs. Even from this distance the town has a festiveness smothered in its shadows. A bee-like hum of gladness surrounds it; the valley sand-bed is walking with lights. They cluster like fireflies through the gate and dance in dim shafts upon it; they throw tall shadows on the city walls. The houses are swathed in a dim luminous halo, except in windows where small bright spots move swiftly. From Sultan 'Ali's palace, a pool of darkness, rifles flash reddish and green. The sound takes a second or two to reach us, while already its light has faded: and each dull explosion is greeted by thin voices of invisible people cheering in the town.

❖   ❖   ❖

The expression of their faces in the Hadhramaut is amiable, hatred is common, but bad temper is scarcely known. The faces of the men are often spoiled by theology, or by being puckered for years in the sun; but the women keep into old age an expression of calmness and sweetness, and the lines that are common in Europe are hardly to be found in these harims. This comes, I think, because, living always together and under a rigid code of courtesy, the feelings which create these lines are never allowed free play. Better than self-control, they have that true serenity which begins at the very source, eliminating those feelings for which self-control is required. I think it is because of this inner quietude that the faces of nuns, of Quakers, and of Arab women have, as they settle into age, the same look of peaceful acceptance and repose.

❖   ❖   ❖

There is some merit in seeming better than you are, an improvement induced by Art on the raw material of Nature; to be better than you seem is merely to inflict on fellow creatures shortcomings which do not even exist.

❖   ❖   ❖

Salih, the youngest of the Children of Muhsin, came and helped me to diagnose a woman who complained of a Sikin in her head. The Sikin is invisible except to a few exceptional people like Salih's father; it has a human form, though much taller, and can live in any substance – a stone, a wall, a door-post – and if you laugh at it, it creeps into you and hurts; if, on the other hand, it – or rather she – likes you, she will come and shake your clothes when you are ill, and bring one or other of the Prophets to cure you. Some Sikins pray and some do not. If she dislikes you, she spits as you pass (spitting is terribly popular) and you come out in a rash. It is very difficult to know her, because she goes about veiled like any other woman, even when she is visible. I thought Epsom salts might discourage her as much as anything; if they did not, I told the woman, Allah would do the rest, and Salih and I continued to discuss the matter after she left. He did not think it was a Sikin, but rather a Barkin, who – or which – is altogether milder and enters like a little cool wind by the great toe of the right foot; it then settles in the chest, swelling in lumps either in front or on one side, and it eats your food, so that you eat and eat and are always hungry. The Wali in the tomb down below can drive it away, out by the big toe as it came.

❖   ❖   ❖

We are in a proud country still new to Europeans, the first foreigners to live in its outlying districts for any length of time; and the hope that I cherish is that we may leave it uncorrupted, its charm of independence intact. I think there is no way to do this and to keep alive the Arab's happiness in his own virtues except to live his life in certain measure. One may differ in material ways; one may sit on chairs and use forks and gramophones; but on no account dare one put before these people, so easily beguiled, a set of values different from their own. Discontent with their standards is the first step in the degradation of the East. Surrounded by our mechanical glamour, the virtues wrung out of the hardness of their lives easily come to appear poor and useless in their eyes; their spirit loses its dignity in this world, its belief in the next. That this unhappy change may come here as elsewhere is only too probable; but it will be no small winter's achievement if it does not come through *us*.

❖   ❖   ❖

The perpetual charm of Arabia is that the traveller finds his level there simply as a human being; the people's directness, deadly to the sentimental or pedantic, likes the less complicated virtues; and the pleasantness of being liked for oneself might, I think, be added to the five reasons for travel given me by Sayyid Abdulla, the watchmaker: 'to leave one's troubles behind one; to earn a living; to acquire learning; to practise good manners; and to meet honourable men.'

❖   ❖   ❖

It is in this heart of our philosophy that we amateurs disagree with your unmitigated expert, whose object is so supremely important that he cannot count, or at any rate notice, the jostling and hurting of others. Beside the pure acetylene of science, the souls of men are apt to look like glow-worms. To be too drowned in business to smile upon a child; or take the long way round because the shorter might corrupt some native mind or heart; or end the tired day with half an hour's pleasantness for others tired

109

as oneself – wrapped in one's own affairs – to move solitary among earth's pilgrim-crowd of strangers – it seems to me that no finding of stones or oil or treasure will compensate this fundamental emptiness.

❖   ❖   ❖

'Shortly before you first came to Hureidha,' Mansur went on, 'my brother was shot dead from the house opposite ours in the palm grove, and we had the blood feud to carry on, and it was inconvenient because the door of each house could be shot at from the windows of the other. Then two years ago Sayyid Abu Bekr, may Allah widen his breast (with happiness), made a truce of four years between us and, from his own purse, gave me a hundred dollars bakhshish for my brother's death. And now the English peace has come, and the blood feud has ceased with no disgrace to me, and it is pleasant, for I and my next-door neighbour can walk together side by side and neither need shoot the other. Thanks be to God.'

❖   ❖   ❖

In the afternoon came the Qadhi with a new manuscript and presently, talking of this and that, told me that he thought of opening a small shop in Hureidha, 'for the passing of time.'

'What will you sell in it?' I asked.

'I have not yet thought of that,' said he, drawing a small sheet of paper from his breast. 'But I have begun by writing a poem to hang by the door on the day that it is opened. I will read it to you. It is the shop, you must understand, that is represented as offering a welcome to its customers.'

❖   ❖   ❖

We have been to lunch, Alinur and I, with the oldest man in Hureidha. I found him sitting in the dust of our kitchen floor, left there by Qasim, who is in love just now and quite unreliable, and he asked us to lunch with him today. His shoulders stoop under a greasy coat of silk striped red and yellow; his cheeks are sucked in with age; his eyes, still embellished with kohl, are flecked green and blue like the sea on a windy day, and his beard is dyed with henna. There is nothing left of him but a sort of ghost-like shell of antique gaiety, the flicker of a candle almost dead. He has been a traveller in his day, and knows South Africa and India and Malaya, and is rich and respected, and has had, it is said, fifty-five wives. He is a friend of all the British who come his way. On the doorstep of his great square house he was waiting to receive us, and deposited us with his wife, a middle-aged woman and plain, who quickly poured her troubles in my ears.

'I hate him, and I have pains all over.'

'That comes from sitting in draughts,' I said, separating the propositions which she seemed to consider as one.

She brushed this aside. 'Who would not feel ill with a husband of ninety-five?' said she.

'You have a beautiful house,' I tried to distract her.

'Pah, and he keeps all the keys and never lets them out of his grasp'; and just at that moment the old man returned, with a plate of ginger in one ancient hand and in the other, a ruby ring on its little finger, the bunch of keys.

The wife retired, we sat on the floor round an excellent meal, and friends and servants who had come to help with the ceremony entertained us with stories of our host. His age is the pride of the town. But he himself sat silent, his light eyes in some dream long past, and presently began to talk quietly of Nairobi and Cape Town and the far-away travels of his youth.

We had been rather surprised to hear that he was building a house at the other end of Hureidha. I asked him about it.

'It is my tomb,' said he. 'It will soon be finished.' His old eyes closed in the middle of our conversation and he was asleep.

'He is old,' said the guests for the twentieth time: 'the oldest man in Hureidha.'

⬦ ⬦ ⬦

... a room completely carpeted with black and silver-spangled female forms. As we advance towards the hostess, friendly hands put our feet into invisible spaces; people we know smile through the deafening clamour: conversation is impossible. The Mansab's wife, a kind plain woman, resplendent in striped brocade, has bells on her toes and anklets, and a mane of silver bells from her coral head-dress to her shoulders: in a gratified murmur which ripples through the loudness of the talking, she rises to dance to her guests. The Singer of Hureidha beats the drum called *hajir*, which has red patterns painted at each end; her eyes are done with kohl in a theatrical line that sweeps to the temple and gives her an idol look. Other women beat small drums about the size and shape of a man's collar-box: they hold them shoulder-high and look at each other with delighted faces in the appalling noise. Among the general black, the sayyid ladies stand gorgeous in colour. The Mansab's sister is near me, pinning false plaits with silver hooks over each ear to help out her own shorter hair in the dancing.

'Don't you get giddy?' I shout as she totters back after the performance.

'You should not ask,' said she. 'It is not thought well to feel giddy – but I do all the same.'

⬦ ⬦ ⬦

When we came home I pressed a few plants I had collected and asked Husain, still ecstatic from his ride, to put a heavy box on the books with which I covered them.

'That is impossible,' said he.

I thought he meant it was too heavy, and said: 'Nonsense.'

'But,' said Husain, 'one should not put anything on top of a book. The word of God may be inside.'

⟡ ⟡ ⟡

The assembling of facts is a means only; the collector is no more master of his universe than the paving stone is master of the road: he makes it indeed for freer feet to tread. It would be ungrateful to despise his devout and necessary labour; but it is also singularly unfair to limit the majesty of science to so pedestrian a track, and to take from it those ecstasies of the imagination which alone transmute the dead array of facts.

In this more vivid rank I do not believe that art and science intrinsically differ. The data of the one are certainly no less accurate and no less indispensable than the other, though less tangible. Too elusive for the instrument of language, *they must be gathered by every maker for himself,* and the labourer and the creator, often separate in science, in art must ever be combined.

⟡ ⟡ ⟡

The spring was everywhere. Intangible yet, it lurked like a promise in the sharpness of the air, in the milky transparency of the sky, in the buzzing of an early bee and the faint pink pea-flowers that sprang from small bushes in the sand. It washed with a secret beauty the brown town on its brown hill-side, and threw its fugitive illusion even on the ancient ramparts of the wadi, making their implacable outline tremulous in the soft arms of air. Life, that mysterious loveliness, was moving; and even the sandy wastes flutter and stir as she passes.

⟡ ⟡ ⟡

There round the walis' tombs they gathered, and then scattered, visiting their own familiar dead. It is a fine sense of drama that so brings them in holiday attire to mingle their small living handful with the unobtrusive headstones, unwalled and uncounted – a recognition of Life

113

and Death, inextricably neighboured. In that wide mortal space about the domes, the smallness of our town became apparent, its inhabitants so largely scattered in the world. For a day or two they have thrown aside the remembrance of their poverty, hanging ever on the sheer edge of starvation . . .   HUREIDHA

❖   ❖   ❖

One cannot deny that civilization has ever been based on the vicarious use of other people's lives.

❖   ❖   ❖

There are, I sometimes think, only two sorts of people in this world – the settled and the nomad – and there is a natural antipathy between them, whatever the land to which they may belong. Perhaps it is because we are comparatively recently barbarians, because the stone age lingered longer among us than on the Mediterranean coasts, that the English have remained so frequently nomadic at heart. It is the more imaginative attitude in a transitory world, where a man who tries to feel settled must appear to the eyes of eternity very like someone pretending to sit in comfort on an ant-hill. And the nomads are without doubt the more amusing. With a mind receptive to the unexpected they acquire a Social Sense. The roughest bedu has it, and it is this that so happily distinguishes him from a peasant like Ahmed or even from a Banker, people who walk through landscapes with their heads down, thinking out sums. The nomad, moving from place to place in mind as well as body, is ready to take an interest in any odd thing that meets him; this makes him pleasant and I am inclined to think it is better to be pleasant than to be virtuous, if the two *must* be looked upon as mutually exclusive.

❖   ❖   ❖

The Oriental idea expressed by St. John that Chaos is the beginning of all things except Speech is true in a lesser way of Arab journeys. By the middle of next morning signs of bustle began like small waves to lap around us, a last effort to extract money was made by all who could force an entry to my room, and at two o'clock Sultan Husain saw me on to a camel which knelt in the dust, in sight of the roofs and battlements and ladies of 'Azzan.

❖   ❖   ❖

This art of theirs of the caravan is the one thing the Arab has learned by endless repetition to do supremely well. One after one all my modern gadgets failed me; the thermos broke, the lunch basket was far too complicated, only the Mansab's quilt stood me in good stead. But the bedu's waterskin, with one hand used as a cup and a funnel, is economical and light; his coffee-pot, brass and unbreakable, hangs under the saddle over the camel's tail; his cotton shawl can be used for everything in the world that cloth is ever used for. He has all that is necessary and nothing superfluous; and if his rope were of the kind that did not break whenever you pull at it, one might say that his equipment was perfect of its kind.

❖   ❖   ❖

The camel is an ugly animal, seen from above. Its shoulders slope formless like a sack, its silly little ears and fluff of bleached curls behind them have a respectable, boarding-house look, like some faded neatness that dresses for propriety but never dressed for love.

❖   ❖   ❖

As we rode I watched the camel before me, admiring the perfection of its desert ways. Its ugliness is the ugliness of the east, that has some strange attraction; its colour is the colour of desert dust, with the same innumerable, imperceptible variations; its tail, which looks like a dead palm frond, is merely ridiculous. But its feet are so strong that I have seen a camel, fully laden, raise itself up on a foot *that was twisted beneath it*, apparently without noticing,

115

and so delicately made, with concertina-like springs at the heel, that they give themselves without shock to every inequality of ground. I can see why the beduin love their camels: they are the only beasts of burden whose constant wish is truly to oblige. Like one of those unselfish people who are always gently moaning, the camel does all that is asked of it with a constantly negative mind: but it does try to do it, and when the bedu shouts 'tariq' from behind, will leave the morsel of green leaves hanging on a branch in mid-air and find obediently the track from which it strayed. Only sometimes, when another caravan comes by, you will hear a vague, individual rumble from a male as he passes, while the lady whom he will never meet again turns to look distantly at him, as if through invisible lorgnettes.

⟡   ⟡   ⟡

'Donkeys,' said Salim, 'are bad animals. The camel, when its master falls, is sorry: but the donkey laughs in its heart.' The braying of the ass is always called laughing here.

⟡   ⟡   ◆

In the dust of the valley, amethyst evening tufts of smoke were rising. Shepherdesses trailed home with the patter of their flocks behind them. This is perhaps the best joy of the journey, to come at evening to your unknown resting-place. However many the disillusions you have left behind you, no habit blunts the thrill of this unknown. The little village, swathed in its own life as in a veil, lies waiting there like a bride before you: and one cannot but feel that it is a passion for mystery chiefly which explains the optimism of human beings towards both polygamy and travel.   ZAHIR

⟡   ⟡   ⟡

Dark indeed must the heart be that does not lift at the sight of the journey's goal set out before it; and I have often thought that, if one lived well, such perhaps may be the hour of death.

❖ ❖ ❖

We have little cargo but thirty-two passengers, who pay three rupees each to be taken a hundred miles to Shuqra. They are mostly beduin and are sick decently over the side. The Sultans have sent eighteen people gratis, to the skipper's annoyance. Nearly all have done the journey by land, which takes ten days; and lying on the deck and thwarts, a thick carpet of bodies wrapped in *futahs* with naked shoulders, they make a running commentary on the landmarks of the shore where, far away in the haze, the familiar and for the moment unattractive shapes of volcanoes appear. The hours go peacefully. The crew sit about, plaiting ropes of palm leaf to sell in Aden for the making of seats. The skipper is pounding henna to dye his beard. At intervals they catch fish on a hook baited with wuzifs, trailed at the end of a long line. They are pulled swishing like silver firework, through the water, and, cooked on a primus stove among the cordage, are divided fairly between us all. The skipper feeds his passengers altogether on rice. There is a cheerful gong sound too on the deck, of ginger beaten in a mortar, to flavour the coffee which at intervals goes round. For me he has brought out his only tin of figs preserved in syrup, given him, he says, by the Italians, and pours out glasses of tea with a sailor's neatness, stirring with the handle of the teaspoon, so as to keep the other end dry for sugar, a thing no land Arab would bother to do.

It must be indelicate to eat in public. When the moment comes, a sail is brought and arranged like a curtain around me. But there are other moments for which no provision is made. The only sanitation are two small wooden cages, tied with rope to the outside of the dhow; here at intervals travellers stay meditating, their lower halves decently hidden, but the rest all exposed to the general view. This publicity I could not face and at last

117

put the problem to the Nakhuda, who looked as if he had been a family man many times over. He saw my point and sent for three oars and a sail; these were draped like a tent, and there I could retire precariously over an ocean that rushed with great speed below, and with some reluctance, since, as I could not monopolize one-half of the sanitation altogether, the tent had to be erected afresh every time. There are inherent difficulties in the situation of a solitary female on a boat.

❖   ❖   ❖

At three in the morning the lighthouse of Aden first appeared, a dim shaft on the hungry ridges, blossoming like civilization in recurrent intervals, with darkness large between. Only from the outer ocean and the night can you know how small a light it is, how vast the currents through which it beckons, how indomitable in his perpetual ventures the spirit of man.

As I lay there, drawing nearer, I thought of this civilization and of the bedu who is so happy without it. Perhaps it is because he need never choose the *second best*. Poor as his best may be, he can follow it when he sees it, and that is freedom. We, too often compelled to see two roads and take the worse one, are by that fact enslaved. Our lesser road may in itself be better than the wild man's best one; but that is neither here nor there, it is our *choice* of the second that makes us second-rate. The second-best for security in finance, the second-best for stability in marriage, the second-best for conformity in thought – it is our civilization, though not that of Hellas nor of the City of God; and every time we consciously accept it our stature is diminished. It would be pleasant, I reflected, to look back on a life that has never given its soul for money, its time to a purpose not believed in, its body to anything but love. The Arab can still say this, unconscious of alternatives. He will take a bribe gladly but will then do what he likes notwithstanding; his servitude does not penetrate far. Even 'Ali, regardless of the rules of property to an

118

inconvenient degree, keeps his inner self free of them in an original way, which the materialist will never understand. The materialist too often is civilized man. Perhaps it is to get away from him, that so many quiet people like to travel in Arabia.

East is West

1939–45

Who has not stood at times in front of some old picture, and imagined himself walking into the artificial stillness of its landscape? It comes to life as he advances into imaginary distance; the donkey trots with panniers in the foreground, the little boy with stick perpetually lifted brings it down with a whack. Fresh dust is on the ruts of that track that winds into the background by towns perched there on small and naked hills. The painter has put them in clearly, one by one, diminishing as the track winds in smaller perspective; in his faithful rendering you can see specks of people – men with sashes and rifles, teams of oxen ploughing in the fields. You can see the Emir descending from his castle, by a steep path that cuts diagonally to the small town below; the chestnut pony whisks its long tail, his bodyguard are running all about him. Smoke rises; the tiny whitewashed windows look out like eyes of owls from their dark walls; sparse trees are dotted in the fields. Something is always happening in this landscape; one can see the brown kites wheeling, one can hear their sweet shrill voices and the rush of their descending wings; one can hear the many little voices from the town; for the fact is that it is not a painting at all, but the everyday, incredible landscape of Dhala.   Nᴿ ADEN

❖   ❖   ❖

If one climbs the mountain beyond Dhala, the rocky mass of Jihaf, 7,800 ft. high, one can see the whole land with its pointed hills and tiny settlements, a tomb of Job on a summit two days westward, and the little square towers that sit on every height. They are built of cubes of dark stone whose varied colour gives them an iridescent look; and they have rough fortified devices, shotholes and machicoulis and embryo battlements. They sit as if stitched in tapestry on the summits of rocks in this pastoral highland whose scanty grass has died away in summer. The unshod ponies climb like cats over the tilted slabs;

123

the tiny harvests make yellow patches stacked in trees or
rocky holes; from their small forts the few inhabitants
gather to watch us ride. Great cacti grow here like taber-
nacle candles, raising clusters of straight prickly shafts
higher than a man on horseback, and the air is as sharp
and pure as the cry of an eagle. Here from this summit of
the principality one looks across to the wall of Yemen,
where withered streams are trickling far below.

❧   ❧   ❧

Officials everywhere labour under a disadvantage in
their pursuit of Good: from their beginning their eyes are
fixed on other bureaucrats' promotions; stimulus and not
nourishment is their daily food. When an artist looks aside
to watch other people's rewards, he ceases to be an artist:
the official in a country where salaries are not high, is
offered no other incentive at all.

The Arab virtues anyway are warm and human and not
very official virtues. To be hospitable and polite in the
extreme, to give money for the good of one's soul regardless of its destination, to further the welfare of all one's
family and friends: – these are excellent virtues, but if
anything they are embarrassing rather than otherwise to
a young bureaucrat.

❧   ❧   ❧

The fact of the matter is that your colonial officer has
the task of a parent multiplied a hundredfold – the
task of an *adopted* parent who has no family likeness to
help him. Adoption in the first place may or may not
have been justified; fortresses like Aden, or Bermuda for
that matter, are destined sooner or later for adoption by
the inherent inequalities of things; that, anyway, has not
been the affair of the colonial official. He does not take up
the burden, but he has to see that it is faithfully borne, and
in doing so has to wrestle not only with the character of
the child itself, but with the voices of all its relations, from
Philanthropy to Big Business, many of them influential and

most of them wrong. If he were an angel from heaven, he could not please them all; but he is an average human being, striving to fit a foreign civilization on to limbs never disciplined to such restrictive garments. And if he is a British official, he comes from a tiny plot which has spread the Idea of itself, at one time or another, over a good part of the habitable earth; the grown-up children are self-supporting with families of their own; they have no central obligation, except in time of war (and then only voluntarily): the colonial official deals only with the young ones, and the parental income is necessarily divided into small morsels to feed so many mouths. They are mostly poor or backward places (otherwise they would be well on the way to cease from being colonies); and every school, road, water-supply or other public work must either be cajoled from the parent chest or achieved out of local resources.

❖   ❖   ❖

It may be asked why, in all these centuries of Oriental sleep, the young Effendi should only now awaken, like a mass-produced version of the Sleeping Beauty? Who has kissed him? Like a modern beauty who is rarely content to be awakened by one Prince only, I should say that the Effendi has responded to at least three: the internal combustion engine, the (mostly) American educator, and the British Government.

If it is plausible to say that the continuance of the American federation was secured by the invention of railways, and that of the British Commonwealth by the invention of aeroplanes, it is equally probable that the aeroplane and the motor-car together may secure the future cohesion of Arabia. The existence of its governments, from the days of Asshur and Sheba to our own, has always depended on security of transport for the long and fragile lines of caravans; and civilizations such as that of Palmyra have vanished like the smoke of a nomad's fire, when some internal tumult or foreign inroad – which

125

would be temporary in lands of a different geography – have snapped the policing and control of the camel tracks, even for a week. Now with mechanical transport neutralizing the desert and linking securely the great oases that form the Arab nations, the young man with a good education becomes more important than a chieftain of the tribes.

❖   ❖   ❖

In the great temples of Egypt the huge stone figures stand, and beside them, no more than knee-high, the figures of their wives. I think it is rather a depressing picture of conjugal relations, but it is an excellent type of the Idea, gigantic beside the smallness of the Man, and a model to all politicians. Perhaps it is because this relation is maintained, the agent so little visible, the idea so great beside him, that the structure of the Catholic Church has stood so many centuries unimpaired. It is the lesson women learn, who hold all heaven in their hands for someone at some moment, and must watch the power depart. It is this knowledge that marks the divergence of statesman and politician; and the tradition of government must teach it, if it teaches anything at all. The man is nothing, the idea he wields everything: it is the chief lesson which the Effendi, coming newly to govern, has to learn.

❖   ❖   ❖

In the late afternoon, in the golden light, we reached the Syrian border and the cities of the dead were about us, and the strange beauty of Asia who makes her ornament of the secrets of her past. A beauty that relies, like a Paris gown, on subtle line with a single knot or ribbon, a trifle of decoration, a broken column in the barren cup of hills, a lad with black goats browsing, a lonely tree, to give the desired note. Style, I suppose it is, both in the French costume and the Syrian landscape – to renounce all but the essential, so that the essential may speak.

❖   ❖   ❖

For the art of conversation, it is an advantage, I think, to belong to a small nation in normal times. There is a detachment, an ease of letting the gaze wander, over the audience, over the platform, anywhere it likes, while the Exalted – banked up there with bouquets – can hardly screw their necks to right or left. The Exalted can only be happy or amusing if they refuse to take themselves seriously, and how few of them do. What was more insufferable than the Victorian manner abroad? Now, in the Middle East, we watch the British grow less rich and far more pleasant, but the Americans begin to share unpopularity; there is no getting away from it; it comes of sitting on the platform.

❖ ❖ ❖

The language of salesmanship was no doubt born with the first fashions in fig leaves in the garden of Eden. A strange concept has grown around it: if something is to be sold, inaccuracy is not immoral. Hence the art of advertisement – untruthfulness combined with repetition. The cliché and the slogan appear, people hear a familiar sound, and take it for granted to believe. What we have not yet fully realized, is the depth to which this salesmanship language has crept into the spiritual realm, into politics, religion, and even art. It is a blot on any civilization; for words are poor enough anyway to express the thoughts behind them, and only the most devoted care can make them even approximately exact: to think lightly of their perversion leads to a perversion of the thought, and hence to cataclysms, war and death.

❖ ❖ ❖

The same sort of person who likes the Arab, likes the Irish, or Italian, or the Greek for that matter; they respond to something that is unregimented and individual, that discovers a reluctance in organizing its soul for worldly good. The people who do *not* like them, who incline to the regulated and German way, are apt to

127

call these people inefficient: but they *are* efficient, only they think that other things are often more worth while. So do I. The call of Efficiency is being sounded all the world over, and, like medicine, is good in reasonable doses; one can only hope that pleasant people may not be addicted to it to the exclusion of all else.

❖   ❖   ❖

Manners indeed are like the cypher in arithmetic – they may not be much in themselves, but they are capable of adding a great deal to the value of everything else.

❖   ❖   ❖

After 1940, whatever the feeling for her policies may have been, the French *complexion*, in those lands whose culture she has kneaded, remained practically unimpaired. I have wondered if British influence would so survive the loss of Britain herself? And, speculating on the cause of this tenacity, believe it to lie in the fact that *ideas* have an importance to Frenchmen which in Britain they lamentably lack. If you place him between a theory and a locomotive, there is small doubt which the average Englishman looks upon as the more substantial; the Frenchman recognizes and serves the intangible, and lives at ease in a house not built with hands.

❖   ❖   ❖

'The merit of the British,' Faris al-Khuri said to me, sitting at his desk with eyes twinkling, 'is that wherever they govern they have *trouble*. They teach freedom, and naturally that makes everybody restless, since one learns to wish to be free. Other countries keep well away from it, and their people are obedient and quiet – like the dead.'

❖   ❖   ❖

Tyre, on her headland, listens to the waves. Her columns are lost or carried away or lie in the sea where they fell broken, and the water, clearer than glass, lisps over them or under, singing an old song learned in the mornings of Time; and the causeway built by Alexander is flanked with fields and crops; and the streets and markets, leisurely places, keep the Roman rectangular shape unwittingly, and the forgetful children of the Phoenicians still build small clumsy boats on the open beaches. There is nothing left in Tyre except this forgetfulness, a life of little things quieter than silence, an essence of oblivion woven with the sun and sea.

❖   ❖   ❖

In spite of the traffic of the greater harbours, Haifa and Beirut and Jaffa, this remote atmosphere clings to the Philistine and Phoenician coasts. As you go south from Athlit you meet it in sun-bleached coves, where villages that once were little cities look down from the ridge of Palestine on to their bays. You find it drifting with the sand and the swallows in and out of the Gothic arches of Tartous; and in Latakia, where sailing ships are moored to shafts of columns sunk into the grass-grown quays; and in Ruad the island of sponges where Phoenician walls, half eaten away, stand on sea-wet ledges, like Titans made undistinguishable by time. All these cities have somewhere in their neighbourhood the ruin of some yet older city: through languages now forgotten or unknown, they go back to days before the record of language: their tombs, their rude cyclopean gateways, their earliest caves in the limestone, make a strange, silent tumult to the mind; and all along this coast the sea wind, and the smooth waves with their undertone and the humming particles of sand seem to exult with a fiercer gaiety than elsewhere, with a ruthless loveliness, constantly triumphant over the works of men.

❖   ❖   ❖

That September month in London was singularly beautiful. It hung like a golden apple on a bough, soon to be detached. The sun, through windless days, shone on the cherubic aluminium roundness of the tethered barrage balloons. They floated benevolently passive, silver at noon, rosy like air-islanded Alps in dawn or sunset. Beneath them was a clearness and a stillness – not the silence that lies in the midst of the havoc of war, the silence found for instance last year in deserted North African vineyards – but a waiting stillness, the majestic pause and gathering together of all that is about to be destroyed. So London waited, sunning itself in the gold of falling leaves, a city of the young and the useful, for the old and the children had then mostly gone away. . . . People walked with their gas-masks slung like cameras over one shoulder, pleasantly in the daylight or with difficulty in the darkness of the first blackout. The searchlights lay like swords above the silhouetted battlements of chimneys. When the moon shone, the parks with their billowing trees, now open to the public, took on an eighteenth-century loveliness of ballet; but at midday, in all the neighbourhoods of White-hall, they were filled with open-air lunchers, clustered in ever-growing swarms . . .

❖ ❖ ❖

Aleppo's darkness seemed remote from the rigid black-out of Europe. The old city wrapped herself in it as in a veil, lifting from swathes of shadow the sloping stones of her glacis and Saladin towers to the moon. The blank walls of the well-built Syrian houses, the tunnelled arch-ways of the suqs, were as they had been through all the ages before progress touched them with electric light – obscure, full of questions; the daytime's contours had melted into some uncatalogued infinity of night. The dim blue lights seemed right here, for they showed what had always been shown – a stretch of wall, a pool of arch, some head-enveloped figure walking on sandalled feet . . .

❖ ❖ ❖

On the morning of July the 8th, 1941, I drove with Sophie Shone to say good-bye to General Wavell. He was being sent away from us, as C.-in-C. to India, after directing four victorious campaigns through four countries and in two continents, and evacuating our army from Greece with twelve aeroplanes and a handful of troops. He looked tired, and sad, and kind, and the huge and empty aerodrome, the sandy edges of the hills, the pale colour-wash – ochre and blue – of the early day, seemed all to lie attendant as a frame to a picture, round the group of uniforms and the weather-beaten faces, and the solitary figure who was handing over the defence of all this world and what it meant. He stopped first with one then another, leaving a trail of affection unspoken but glowing, warmer than the pale sunshine of the morning. Admiral Cunningham and some of the Navy were there, and a few Air Force with our new A.O.C.-in-C., Sir Arthur Tedder, a great leader and a charming human being; and Lady Wavell and two daughters, and Peter and a number of the Army. The little group, the buff and scarlet and gold, lonely in the bright morning where only the kites were flying, with the camouflaged Lysander lying like some French brig ready to take off into the sea of air, made me think strangely of a Highland farewell in the Stuart wars; the image was not inspired by any thought of lost causes, but by an atmosphere of loyalty and personal devotion that hung about the scene, and with it an acceptance of all that comes. Sometimes it is given one to see men greater than all their fates, through some accidental rift, as it were. Here it was perhaps the loneliness of the sandy aerodrome where so little coming and going of aircraft lay at our command: the handful of men who stood there were holders of the bridge of Asia: General Sir Claude Auchinleck, with his fine head like a lion, had his foot already upon it; the watch on the bridge was being changed: and far away the landscapes of Asia and Africa, widening from their meeting places, the ranges and deserts and ranges, and pale green intersecting valleys, lay waiting; and the pincer claws of the enemy, at which in their advance we were so desperately hacking, were beyond, on the horizon of the Caucasus, of Libya and of Crete. All this was visible, if one looked, on Heliopolis aerodrome that morning.

❖ ❖ ❖

The skipper stood on the tiny bridge below, obeying orders as they flashed from *Leander*, our cruiser in the van. He suggested that I had better take cover in the cabin, purely as a matter of form, and so I disregarded it. On the smooth sea, gay in the morning sunlight, the varied convoy ploughed its way as if in lines of traffic; we came to have a feeling of affectionate comradeship for the ships immediately ahead or astern, whose movements had to harmonize with ours. The destroyers on our flanks swept about us, sharp-snouted as swordfish, and the sea banked in a green wall behind them, after the hissing foam. And now the raiders came, flying very high, ten thousand feet or more, deep in the gulfs of the sky; it seemed to wash over and hide them with its thin blue waves. They came like gods of the Iliad into battle, swift and unattainable, and huge cones of water leaped from their bombs around our cruiser, as high as the masts above her funnel, and the quiet, secret, sunny depths of the sea were wrenched and stunned with explosions, Poseidon, that slow god, attacked in his realm. Then I saw the most majestic sight that anyone could witness, for *Leander* answered with all her guns. The great ship was wrapped in a single garment of flame yellow and shining in the sun; so must Athene with her shield have appeared in the forefront of battle.

❖ ❖ ❖

The Marshes are some thirty to forty miles wide along the Persian border and over a hundred miles long from north to south – an enchanted country, unlike anything else in the world. Their reeds grow in clear deep water only, as much as forty feet high. They enclose broad ways and narrow windings, known to the amphibious Arab, and sudden lakes where the water flowers heave gently, an indolent carpet brightly woven, over the wash of the canoe. The traffic of the border goes by these waterways, and the men of the boat caravans will bend the reeds into platforms for their nightly camp, and build fires upon them, islanded in the rustling loneliness. On a day in spring when this water-land blossoms, it is a sort of Paradise untouched by man. The black tarrada, the swan-necked canoe studded with painted, black, large-headed nails to make it strong, slips with only the drip of its oars through sunlight seamed with a myriad shadows criss-crossing in the heart of the reeds, through silences that listen to a myriad noises, the dive of the white and black kingfishers, the scurry of a moorhen, the hum of small flies or mosquitoes (luckily not malarious) in the sun; and everywhere, always, the sharp-leaved rustle of the reeds, bending and singing, closing as one pushes through the yielding stems, or opening away to the clearing of a short horizon, a gentle, cruel, inexorable prison to those who have not learnt the maze of the ways. Their charm is loneliness, the opening of a door, the sharing of a secret with a world that is as it was and will be, before and after the visitings of men. IRAQ

❖　❖　❖

Baghdad has the romance of the Golden Road, of a city on the route of caravans; Mosul has memories of Assyria and a rugged enchantment of the north; but Basra is the Ocean door of Arabia, rich, buoyant, adventurous, enter-prisingly-minded, easy of intercourse, speaking even today the language that Drake and his friends could understand. As you sail up her broad breast of waters from Fao, you can see the palaces of her merchants surrounded by flowering creepers, shaded by palms, painted and carved with wooden Gothic ornamented pillars, where the rich men spend their leisure with a fictitious coolness of water lapping in their ears.

❖　❖　❖

The lovely Persian spring lay like an embroidered mantle on the hills; larks were beating their small cymbals in the sun, unseen; from the flowery pasture waves of scented air broke like invisible foam about the speeding car. . . .

❖   ❖   ❖

Wherever the Arab civilization reigns, the spirit still triumphs over circumstance, and the most unlikely place develops a ceremonial drawing-room atmosphere of leisure.

❖   ❖   ❖

The world, as it grows prosperous, will ever settle in stone, but who shall say what the Nomad is and when he dies? Prometheus' fire, Greek cornices in Parthia, the 'fluid drive' Chrysler in Wadi Tharthar, London bathrooms by the ruins of Asshur – these too are Nomads, products of a spirit as old, as young, as adventurous and as eternal as the minds of men.

Dust in the Lion's Paw

Autobiography 1939-45

... the use of words, with which I am chiefly concerned and with which this book chiefly deals, is at the heart of thought and therefore of action. Attention to it is not to be deferred for times of crisis, since its neglect hatches the crisis in itself. In an age prosperous as this promises to be if violence can be avoided, the importance of words, their management and their reality, becomes supreme. If they are mishandled or abused, even for the simplest purposes, they produce corruption and decay, for it must never be forgotten that they are the vesture of something greater than themselves – doorkeepers to a sanctuary as the evangelist saw them, and as indeed they are.

We have failed in part. And yet we have no wish to recapture the material trappings of a past that has moved on: but during that past, in our need, the spirit of our words did not fail; we held its sharpness by the handle; and nothing but the integrity of what we say and the belief in our saying can give us that handle again in whatever its future may be.

❖　　❖　　❖

A main obstacle was the unfortunate word *propaganda* itself. When first adopted by the Church of Rome it was simply used in the gospel sense of the spreading of a faith, until a reputation for subtlety whether or no deserved gave it a new and sinister twist of deceit. Two opposite ideas, the truth and the hiding of the truth, thus became sheathed in one term, and have been shuffled promiscuously inside it ever since. I soon decided to leave the unhappy word in the climate of its acquired darkness, and to use *persuasion* (for want of a better) to express the spreading of ideas that are genuinely believed. A missionary told me in the middle of the war that she could not take sides because of her religion (the Archangels were less particular, though the occasion had been less ambiguous no doubt); her confusion was, however, I believe, chiefly brought about by language; if the good word *gospel* had been used instead of *propaganda*, her mind would have been clearer, and if some such definition had been generally connected with what our Ministry was saying, we should have realized that it was not only desirable but also honest to distribute our persuasion as truly as we could. There would have been less reliance on statistics of things like pig-iron to make the nations of the world believe that our cause was just. What we were dealing with was the originating and spreading of *ideas*, whose dynamic force, whose almost unlimited consequences, we are so strangely unaware of. In physical disease, international medicine and co-operation promptly intervene; political laws are combated in a lukewarm way merely because most people – and Anglo-Saxons in particular – are unwilling to admit that thoughts can matter; and as these clothe themselves in language, it follows that the importance of words is underestimated too. While originality can be left to a natural variety in nature, truthfulness (one's own attainment of it at all events) is a matter of constant renewal and the only lasting foundation for style. Clear thinking must show behind it. Perhaps nothing but a sacramental attitude – a feeling for the sanctity of utterance in general – will nerve one for the labour. These are vast matters: the whole of civilization is in their orbit; and their neglect made a war possible at a time when most of the world had ceased to believe in it. Seen against such livid consequences, the only excuse for not attempting *persuasion* would be a weakness, a want of knowledge or conviction, in ourselves.

❖   ❖   ❖

A correct estimate of the formidable instrument of persuasion, its legitimate and illegitimate uses, seems to me as urgent as the study of any of the other engines of our day, and the more important since it lies open in the hands of ignorance for any inconsidered rashness. In one form or another, conscious or unconscious, we have all become propagandists; integrity alone can keep us truthful.

❖ ❖ ❖

One has to deal with the agonies of life in literature, but until they are transmitted into their own serene world they are not literature. The people who escape them will never write anything permanent, I suppose; but the *whole* process of transmutation has to be gone through, and the artist must emerge on the other side.

❖ ❖ ❖

How flattering it is for women to be compared to the sea. It may be changeable, but no one could get tired of its playing, every wave different from the last.

❖ ❖ ❖

I always wonder why it should be derogatory to behave like a woman when one is one.

❖ ❖ ❖

The lift girl said to me today: 'Have you seen the *darling* review about you in the paper?' She is such a pretty girl: you would think she ought to know what darling should or shouldn't be used for.

❖ ❖ ❖

If the past were ever past there would be little use in recalling it; but it lives with us in never-ending variation, as if it were a magic carpet on which we travel through the middle air. The contours of our destination were long ago woven in its fading colours and half-obliterated mazes, and the time to alter or improve them passes quickly while the landscapes of our world race by below. Our future is uncontrollable if we are unable to read our past.

❖ ❖ ❖

At the bottom of the turmoil of our time one thing only
– the absence of *truth*: in all parts of human life the importance of truth is now less regarded: it was a love for this
alone that raised Greece to the peak of civilization. To
think of your public rather than of the truth of what you
say is, for instance, quite common and not regarded as a
crime: but it *is* a crime. It means that you flit from point
to point of the circumference while, if you go deeper and
try merely to be true, you find yourself eventually not only
at home in your own centre, but in the universal centre
of all human hearts. Only so by *truthfulness* can we reach
the universal, and therefore a hope of concord among men.

❖   ❖   ❖

The most ominous of fallacies – the belief that things
can be kept static by inaction. Action and inaction are
merely two facets of activity, and when in danger it is
better to hold a sharp knife by the handle rather than so
to blunt it that no one, friend or foe, can find it useful.

❖   ❖   ❖

Patriotism of all things is an emotion one cannot take
for granted, as it would be different if we happened to
have been born inside some other geographic lines. Together with colour, it seems to me to be the most arbitrary
of all human divisions, since pure accident determines
them both: skin has no more relation to one's being than,
say, the eyes or hair; and as for the frontiers in which
we were born, they have mostly been changed a dozen
times in history with all their implications. Yet these
feelings exist: not colour, as far as I am concerned, for
the likeness of human beings strike me far more than their
difference; but the pattern of my own country is very
strong, hammered like metal out of forgotten strokes that
have all left their impact, till the unified surface bears
only a richness, a patina of workmanship, to tell the lives
and centuries through which it was made. Yet the mystery
remains why an irrelevant line drawn by men should

limit our affections, when the same sort of world stretches beyond it. Perhaps it is language, more than any other shackle, that circumscribes our freedom in the family of men?

❖   ❖   ❖

The writing of autobiography is a fragile uprooting – we sift with a constant surprise at finding our life so inextricably interleaved with lives of other people: its complication, in which we are so intimately involved, appears to us three-dimensional against the apparently flat and simple surface of our neighbours. Yet as we unravel our thread we find – there, in the lives that touched us – the origin or echo of every mood we thought of as our own. It is less through us than through *their* alien or divergent mirrors that the light we had in us has been allowed to shine.

❖   ❖   ❖

Life, to be happy at all, must be in its way a sacrament, and it is a failure in religion to divorce it from the holy acts of everyday, of ordinary human existence. The Greeks saw in every drink of water, in every fruitful tree, in every varied moment of their living, the agency of a God.

❖   ❖   ❖

I am sure the first idea of a Turkish mosque came to someone who saw two cypress trees, one on either side of a small round hill. I look out at such a landscape and it is like Saint Sophia with à minaret on either side of the dome.

❖   ❖   ❖

Liberty, the loveliness of Persia, was all about me: those groups of riders, those herds and flocks, the town-free spaces, the limpid air. As I drove along, with my foreboding, uncertain of what the frontier might hold, I thought of all the things good and bad that I had seen in my short journey – the larks and the honey-scented air; the bird in the night; the snow-slopes and poplars of Teheran; a boy with a bicycle, on a boulder in a stream, reading; the errand boy strolling with a bunch of roses; four gazelles crossing the road; the flocks of sheep adrift on the *dasht* like fat summer clouds; black tents where the hill slope breaks like a wave above them; the crescent moon reflected in the stream-bed of a village street, with the old moon in her arm; three villagers round their pool where the little splash could mingle with their talk; fields of blue hyacinths; the shepherd's fire high up on Kuh Parau and the outline of Bisitun rocks under the moon. I thought of Persia sitting like a frog in front of the German python; of the poverty of the people and the ugliness of their clothes; of what some people drank and some of their wives said; and how mixed the world, with a balance on the whole in its favour.

❖   ❖   ❖

I could sleep out in a garden and be wakened in the early morning by a chorale of small birds and by the sun before dawn beating on the underwings of doves. They flew all one way, to or from their morning drink, the shadow of their bodies against half a wing and the rest of them shining in the sky. Beneath them the dates hung like heavy udders round the palm stems – columns in some temple of fertility rather than trees.   BAGHDAD

Ionia

1952

To catch even the echo a thousand times weakened and repeated of the authentic voice of happiness, is worth a journey.

❖ ❖ ❖

I came on deck as we rounded the corner of the gulf of Smyrna. The sea had a satin sleekness of early morning. It lay reflecting, in pale green sheets of brilliance, the splintered red bars of the sky. Behind low hills, still black and closed as buds of flowers, the hidden sun threw up his quills of light. It was the moment when the play begins, when the curtains of the full day are drawn. Out of the smooth sea, in front of the sun, a dolphin leaped full into the air, one fin vertical above his head, and his tail in a curve beneath him. He hung there, as he may have appeared in the shield of Odysseus, as many a Minoan artist saw him, black against the light; and he gave me a shock of ecstasy, as if he were a messenger from the world I was seeking.

❖ ❖ ❖

The Chinese or Persian draughtsman, simplifying his tools, makes the line of a brush or pen sensitive enough to carry the whole weight of his meaning; and I feel this to be the secret also of the Ionian landscape – held in flawless contours and lit by a pure light, and almost independent of detail or of colour.

❖ ❖ ❖

Every reader may decide for himself what part of this world might still be reconstructed in our time. It would be too summary, I think, to assume that none of it can be recovered. The ingredients that made it, as I see them, and as I try to describe them under the names of the various towns of Aeolis and Ionia that follow, were: climate and the healthiest of foods – olives, and fish and corn and wine; leisure, and a simplicity of pleasures; precariousness, to make good moments sharper; and commerce like a river where ideas as well as wealth move up and down. Add to these enough solitude to divide one city or one human being from the next one; curiosity and toleration, which produce truth together; beauty, under whose wing great words are written; a life where personal decisions are demanded; and freedom for women and men. Above all, a tradition that, to be a 'lively oracle', must be surrounded by the Unexpected, friendly to it, and instrinsically honourable in itself: so that in periods of emptiness the symbol may be preserved with piety, ready for a new breath when it comes.

✶ ✶ ✶

Curiosity ought to increase as one gets older. The earth grows bigger, it ceases to contain itself, it laps beyond its sphere; and Time comes less and less to be confined in this tangible air.

✶ ✶ ✶

The respect which curiosity inspires makes it more welcome than charity. It makes us not only in love with, but also interested in our neighbour; and if we cannot be both, then interest is the more important, for that will prevent our doing things for him not in his way but in ours. And curiosity is of course the negation of missionary zeal: for we cannot wish to alter, or do more than move in its own direction the thing we truly care for.

Once divested of missionary virus, the cult of our own gods gives no offence. It would be a peaceful age if this were recognized, and religion, Christian, communist or any other, were to rely on practice and not on conversion for her growth.

✶ ✶ ✶

It is better to be passionate than to be tolerant at the expense of one's soul.

✶ ✶ ✶

Tolerance comes because the attaining of truth is only possible in the sight of things as they are; and things as they are have many facets. She is born out of Uncertainty and Commerce, by Curiosity and Truth. And the mildness of her voice is recognizable at once.

❖   ❖   ❖

One would gladly be independent of commerce, yet the evidence of history seems to mark the transcontinental highways as the thread which the life of the world as we know it must spin.

❖   ❖   ❖

In the family history of the Levant it is strife which has bound the tie so close, holding the family together in a devotion made rigid through centuries of fears. Love is an affair of kindred, a meeting at the same church, a drawing of like to like; it stops at a barrier which Christianity sought in vain to overcome. And its fundamental origin in strife, creating from ancient time the separateness of Greek and barbarian, goes far to explain both the transitoriness and the perfection of that civilization of the dawn.

Most loves in our time also are guarded by strife. The fence of race; the notice at the frontier; the war of class; the team spirit; the party system; not one of these loyalties but Strife around it holds the ring. Shut in from outer clamours, the Mediterranean world established in the family an enclosure of safety. Now the family itself shifts away from Aphrodite, shrinking to an ever smaller nucleus the area of peace. Nor will anything public make good the deficit, since every frontier is doomed to produce an opposition beyond it. Nothing short of the universal can build the unfenced peace.

❖   ❖   ❖

The annexing of wives is the most ancient process by which civilization is preserved: captured women bring their needles and their ovens, their cooking-pots and all

147

the mechanism of domestic life, and cover the hiatus produced by a new set of men. Nothing is more alluring than to follow some single object among these domestic utensils – the pierced stone or piece of clay for instance, that weights the woollen thread as it falls rolled from the hand of the spinner, such as the young nomad girls use today in the mountains of Caria, walking ahead of their camels with the leading string tucked under their arm, spinning as they walk: the same instrument is found in layer upon layer of human habitation, through iron and bronze ages and copper, to the neolithic flint.

❖   ❖   ❖

Perhaps the sixth century of Ionia would never have blossomed if a daily press had then been in existence to deceive with the illusion that Uncertainty is dead. We are drugged to forget how little our strides carry, however stretched they may be; the real position remains almost unchanged since the yardstick is infinity. The modern world has made its foreground definite, with discoveries of science and of fact; but this in itself distorts the picture, since we forget that the foreground is not reality. When less was known the sight travelled farther because the proportion was more accurately kept. Adventure and mystery, perhaps the greatest mortal ingredients of happiness – love being immortal – were not polished away from the surfaces of things by exact but unimportant information. Events came looming full of possibilities as well as fears.

❖   ❖   ❖

A moment may come when we recognize the face of our world, as we mould it, to be death; and we will then think no change too drastic, no renunciation too high, for the recapturing of what once demonstrated, by its actual existence, the infinite possibility in men.

❖   ❖   ❖

By an intrusion of ethics where they are not required, we are put into the absurd position of assuming the Absolute to be within our reach.

❧   ❧   ❧

Like the clear Ionian voice out of obscure mythologies and the groping of mixed peoples, the thin thread of water, the wayfarer's perennial refreshment, came lightly out of the earth.

❧   ❧   ❧

The olive branches were above my head and pushed with a present joy into the sun. Their leaves, brighter than the sky above them, seemed beaten out of metal, so delicate and strong. Where they curled, it was no drooping at the edges, but a general curve all down their length, like a tiny scroll to be held in the hand of a statue. Even in shadow, the rough trunks were warm – scarred and friendly to touch. In its tough beauty, drawn out of the hard pale soil, the olive too seemed to grow for its own pleasure, invulnerable, whoever might collect the fruit – its benefits mere incidents in the self-contained radiance. Harvests, gathered or ungathered, went back, year touching year, into days before the mounded graves of the valley were thought of, before strangers landed from boats at Elaea, days when a nymph could still find safety by being turned into a bear. A silent contemplation, a depth and width uncircumscribed, held all the hill-side in the hot and solitary afternoon: and the harvest, by which so many in so many succeeding ages have been fed, was the least part of the olive tree's secret – an exterior ornament, a shedding during the process of life: like the undying cities, the tree leaves the fruit it scatters to be snatched by whoever comes: the heart of the mystery is its own.

❧   ❧   ❧

On the lake's near side and even paler in the sun than its waters, are the mounds of the Lydian kings. They make a hill landscape of their own, small as a map, on a sloping strip beneath widening mountains, under the same lake-coloured sky. There is no heap so eloquent as a tumulus, for no farewell is quite as definite as that of the grass-growing earth.

❖   ❖   ❖

The valley, noble and open, without craggyness, with ample rounded hills, now began to lift itself as if with deep breaths like a Bach toccata, into higher air. Here and there, against pine hill-sides, poplars made temple-colonnades of gold. The river wound silkily in the sun, far below. The ridges leaned like sleeping nymphs, so gently rounded, wooded or bare; smoke rose high up from the last nomad camps of summer.   APHRODISIAS

❖   ❖   ❖

Lucian describes cities as hives where 'each man has his sting and stings his neighbour'. . . . And though history makes it certain that there was truth in the simile, and though I have little learning to imagine how a Greek city worked in detail, yet I am convinced that I know what the Aeolian mercenary felt as he rounded the promontory which gave the temple of Gryneium and the hill above it to his sight. It was a feeling which had the meaning of geography behind it; not only the city, but all the spaces separating it from all other cities, and all the difficulties of news and of travel were in the sentiment of home: even now, as one sails in a small craft along the loneliness of the more southerly peninsulas of Asia Minor, this feeling catches one in sight of some ragged nestling township in a bay, the evening's goal, although no ties bind one and there is nothing intrinsic to admire – it is an emotion built up out of its contrary emotions, humanity after loneliness, the beauty of a star.

❖   ❖   ❖

The Greek walls whose blocks are finely cut all round so that even what is hidden is beautiful; the backs of

Venetian palaces carved with marble cornices and mouldings on narrow blind canals where no one goes; the Greek siting of their buildings fitted to the unevenness of the land as they found it; the rich cloth that is mended because it cannot be replaced; the road that winds about with the landscape instead of cutting through it, however uneconomic or inconvenient – all these make an intercourse and harmony between two things that contribute to each other, the creator and his creature, the receiver and giver, the artist and his stone.

❖ ❖ ❖

The crash of the whole ancient world was required to make us turn from the city of our fathers to the city of God as Augustine saw it under the darkness of the Vandals. If the world now is to be deprived of both these safeties, we may be poor indeed.

❖ ❖ ❖

What remains of Priene lies high up in the sun. The entry to the theatre is so unobtrusive that one scarcely notices it. Without preparation, it is there. One steps suddenly between the seats and the proscenium, into the orchestra, a small grassy space light with daisies, enclosed in a semicircle where six stone arm-chairs for the most important people are evenly spaced with an altar among them. The seats behind rise in their tiers; the narrow shallow steps of gangways cut them at intervals; and I felt that I was interrupting – that actors and audience, like a flight of shy birds, had fled in the very instant of my stepping across their threshold with my feet still shod in Time. I lingered in the little theatre as if I were a person in the legend, who is given one glimpse of a world which appears to last for seconds only, though all the expanses of time are packed there.

The whole city was built in the flower of the Hellenistic age, and to that its rich austerity belonged.

What was the secret? *Respect* perhaps, so closely tied to

151

love? Respect for what gives itself, and is therefore vulnerable, whether it be a human being or a piece of stone? A gratitude that inspires fastidiousness, a longing to keep intact in its own dignity the object or the being that has helped one to create and to become?

That so subtle a scruple can transmute itself into stone and stay there, is magic; and no conscious effort of the craftsman, nothing but the feeling itself, can leave that mark. Where it exists, it is definite, and every true artist will recognize it across any bridge of time. Without it there is neither sincerity nor greatness. It is a sharing partnership, both giving and taking – a marriage in terms of human life – a tender thankfulness for a benefit received and a forgetfulness of self in the interest of another; and it reaches through the depths of being to that which Heraclitus thought of as Fire and we think of as Love.

❖   ❖   ❖

The people of Priene took their fortune as it came to them, as it comes to us all, out of its great distance. Among their many buffetings, they kept a steady hand, and chiselled in the hard world the record of their life, with that regard for the matter it is made of which renders it beautiful: sure in their human dignity that the greatness of art is not what we have, but what we want and long for, and recognize but never see in men's hearts or in the substances of earth. So they dealt carefully, not smirching with vanity the things they used, but respecting in each its own secret; and transmitted it in stone for as long as the stone may wear.

❖   ❖   ❖

The Persians could now dig away as they liked at our bridge of Miletus, setting their engines to separate them from a world already ancient in their day. When the bridge fell, the discovery of the infinity of man and his universe was safely on our side: Pythagoras and Empedocles,

Athens and Rome, the Fathers of the Church and the philosophers, even to the dividers of the atom, were waiting in their turn to receive and to transmute it; and we have ever felt that the only thing that matters had become safely ours.

But the people of the fifth century saw the whole shining structure of their past go down with Miletus. They could not guess that a few fragments would suffice to feed the future; and they mourned with an anguish that can still be felt. They wept in the theatre in Athens: and when the later Carians looked for allies, the Oracle of Didyma answered them with a cry that still echoes, bitter with desolation, saying that: 'There was a time when the Milesians were brave.'

❖ ❖ ❖

The depth of all we say lies hidden deep under the surface of the words. The fallacy of so-called realism is that it concentrates on illusion; it uses description superficially and not, as the great ages use it, to show from common porches time and eternity implicit in the commonplace. The 'realist' sets description on a pedestal as if it had a reality of its own. This is the art of decadence. The great ages find a more withdrawn reality.

❖ ❖ ❖

It is a quality of great writing that it adapts itself to more than was ever in the writer's mind – and perhaps that too is an illustration of the philosopher's fundamental Unity. But in any case it is a mistake to think, as one is apt to do with the classics, or the Elizabethan English, that some inevitable *luck* made their language; for words are but drops pressed out of the lives of those who lived them.

❖ ❖ ❖

The world has become too full of many things, an over-furnished room. But, to make up for this loss, the immortality of the ancient poets has been lifted out of Time: it is

153

made warm, like a garment, about us: it exists neither afterwards nor now, but always – the kingdom of Heaven, the Boundless of the old philosophers after six centuries of thinking, the house of many mansions, the eternity of the servants of God. Because of it, in spite of sorrow, happiness is the health of the spirit; nor is anything to be counted a disaster except the perversion of the soul.

This legacy must surely live within us; at these cross-roads of the ancient and the later time, far from my physical sight in time and space, but close in my heart, I leave the lands of Ionia – existent, like fairyland, like the kingdom of heaven, supremely beautiful, in and out of our everyday life ever available, yet not often nor easily found.

The Lycian Shore

1954

One is led astray; for how can one neglect a Roman gateway because it is outside one's period, or pass by St. Paul without a word because he travels in a century different from one's own? And then there is the problem of Time, its essence and its limitations.

❖   ❖   ❖

The water as we swam about in it was still and immaterial, so that nothing but space seemed to divide us from the sea-urchins: self-contained in black velvet bristles, they sat scattered like Cyclades or Sporades on the untroubled sand. They appeared, I thought as I floated above them, to have mastered the art of being purely defensive – a thing that was never possible to the Athenians.

Outside our bay but quite near, the ruffle of the wind continued. One could see but not hear it making a noise, running its fingers through the blue and tangling it in waves. Safe in shelter, the *Elfin* gave a tiny movement now and then, of patience, like a sigh, or a horse standing that shifts from one foot to another.

In that leisure, Time became non-existent. To me, at any rate, it seems less real than space, though both are vague enough. The past is never quite past. If the Athenians, so long ago, had acted differently, some ramification, some untraceable divergence would have affected the lives of all of us – even mine, as I swam in the sun. There is a bond of past and future, with us between them, and every act, moving from one into the other, changes the world as it does so. The atomic age has in fact been with us always, since the first deed started the first consequence on its way.

❖   ❖   ❖

I stepped over the stones rattled by earthquakes on their foundations, and climbed from terrace to terrace of corn where the peasants build shallow walls round the pockets of the ancient houses. The full ears, ready for harvest, beat their slight weight against my passing hand, as if they too would spend their weak resistance for the headland's warm and living peace. So remote, so undisturbed was the great hollow, that its own particular divinity seemed to fill it – complete in being as a cup is filled to its brim. There was no judgement here, but only consequence of actions; the good corn filled itself out in deeper places and the bad dwindled among stones, and all things were a part of each other in a soil that someone's building two thousand or more years ago had fattened or spoiled. A fair-haired woman, still beautiful, with green eyes, was reaping. I asked if I might photograph, and she called her husband, who came climbing up and stood beside her, and glanced at her and smiled when I said she was like the English to look at: they were both pleased by her fairness, and there was a happy friendliness between them. He had the oval face of the Mediterranean, and she the straight northern brows: and the history of the world had washed over Cnidus to produce them both, from the days when their ancestors, in the oldest city of the peninsula, joined in building the Hellenium in Egypt, or sent the first caryatid to Delphi.

❖   ❖   ❖

The Greek goddesses, particularly Hera, had much in common with the Victorian idea of women – an idea shared by every age that concentrates on the differences and not on the likenesses of the sexes. It produces chivalry; and it seems to me not altogether a feminine advantage that it has been superseded, and that the similarities are now so much more emphasized than the differences that some women and far too many men seem to be unaware of any divergence at all. The woman's difference turns her into a symbol, a refuge where life is potentially nourished or sheltered, a window out of time, however humble, towards the secret of duration and life.

⬦ ⬦ ⬦

The light seemed to melt, as if it were eating the islands; it lay heavy like the sheaves of a yellow harvest made of air, flattened into wide smooth circles by the sun. A timeless, motionless eternity seemed to hold it; the gossip of the waves, the small white edges breaking, went on unseen below. The same illusion of quietness, the same perpetual motion.

⬦ ⬦ ⬦

The surface of the water was caught by moonlight, as if a crowd of golden sickles were harvesting its darkness.

⬦ ⬦ ⬦

Not only love – each life flows to its moment, of which the greatest art can only be the memory – a gilding that recalls the vanished gold. In their history too the nations reach their climax and lose it; they graze it and drift away, like swimmers in hard waters. Is it stability that they touch in the brief perfection, or does that perfection float rootless, to be met but never to be kept? This must be the chief of all things for students of history to study, and indeed for anyone else who wishes to discover the world as it is.

⬦ ⬦ ⬦

A flock was trickling down the hill-side, in scattered groups like drops towards the stream. It is always the image of the *flock* in the New Testament: no external compulsion holds it, and the partnership of the faithful is never a unity constrained in walls. The closed door is the image used for exclusion or death.

The flock is nothing but a heartfelt direction. It moves to its desire until the unity that guided it is lost or forgotten, and then it falls to pieces too: and locks and walls and the uses of constraint are remembered, administration rules instead of serving, and the closed door becomes an emblem of order: and this not only in the Roman world. But the Greeks, perhaps because of their doubts, kept the free unity – the feeling of a flock that seeks and belongs to the same pastures; and the pattern of their civilization, in the fourth century B.C. and after, came to be a badge no longer of blood but of mind, Hellenic in essence, but not dependent on climate or race. This conquered in the wake of Alexander, and spread through Asia, and tamed the victories of Rome.

Therefore, in spite of order we lament the Roman victories, although in the West we should be exiles without them. For we know that the flock is happiest with its own shepherds; and no external fold, however safe, should hold it long.

❖   ❖   ❖

Time we can neither stop nor start, but only steer: direction only is given us to hold. The source of political trouble lies in this confusion between the mastery and the direction of time. The past is our treasure. Its works, whether we know them or not, flourish in our lives with whatever strength they had. From it we draw provision for our journey, the collected wisdom whose harvests are all ours to reap and carry with us, though we may never live again in the fields that grew them.

❖   ❖   ❖

In the fourth century B.C. the sculpture of the Greek world changed. It acquired movement. Man, no longer firmly planted, was shown with grace and drama shifting his weight from one foot to the other in the act of motion. It is the process of transition which, if uncertain or undirected, becomes a decline: and the human movement is the same. If, as it passes from one step to the next one, the hope, the joy, are lost – the fault is not in the being whose

160

possibilities remain unaltered, but in the goal to which his face is set. The free choice of one age fails in the next, either because its transition is uncertain, or because, out of fear, it does not stir at all; then it stiffens into an obstacle; and the river of time foams over it and destroys it.

⋄ ⋄ ⋄

Classical greatness is *passion*, whether of thought or action – the wholeness of a community, as of an individual, flowing in one direction, without negation or reservation, and in coincidence with Time. This coincidence and this unity give that illusion of stillness which we call serenity; and while the unity with Time remains unbroken, the heroic age continues. The whole business of the statesman and the teacher is to keep these two separate processions, of the human being and of Time, together. And Time, which is rather a vague expression, I take in this connexion to mean all those circumstances which are going on around but are not intrinsically a part of the orbit of a man's life, and with it make up the climate of his age.

⋄ ⋄ ⋄

There can be no happiness if the things we believe in are different from the things we do.

⋄ ⋄ ⋄

The statesman, like the caricaturist, must choose few strokes for his picture and only the ones that matter. It is a difficult, but a simple, task. Direction and pace are his instruments, to keep his age in step with Time, and therefore great; or to speed it up or slow it down, so as to rectify some out-of-step condition of the past and so produce an age of change; or to let it move out of step with its own day – either faster or slower – when the consequence that we call decadence will follow, and the children of his own and many later generations will have to struggle in the cross-currents of decay. Things good in themselves –

161

the tradition of a village or the faith of a Demosthenes –
perfectly valid in the integrity of their origins, become
fetters if they cannot alter. Not permanence but change,
its pace and its direction, are all that matter. The human
creature must shift his weight from one step to the next
one; and to make him do it without either hesitation or
haste is the statesman's task.

No human good that we know is outside our temporal
orbit. Few – very few – of our attainments are so profound
that they are valid for always; even if they are so, they
need adjustment, a straightening here, a loosening there,
like an old garment to be fitted to the body! and men
will submit to this, if they can believe in the rightness of
the aim; for who would not make for his own welfare if
he were *sure*? So Socrates thought, assuming that the good
need only be recognized to be pursued: and the uncertainty of the recognition in his day – the demand for
the search so to say – was the symptom of a discord in
time, produced by unyielding and unadapted loyalties –
patriotism and religion most of all.

Patriotism in particular has ever been thought of as a
sign of the worthiness of nations, preserving them from
being taught in ways contrary to their needs. It saves them
from alien impositions which may put them out of tune
with the reality and produce that vacillation which is the
decadence of nations. It limits them to home-made mistakes. Yet a conqueror can be beneficial, if his aim and
his age agree. History has to roll by to make the process
visible, and the Greeks of the fourth century B.C. scarcely
saw by what steps they were advancing into the larger
unity of Alexander's world. It was not decline but transition – but so confused and hesitating, so clogged by
shibboleths and clichés, that the name of decadence has
often been applied.

❖   ❖   ❖

In the stillness of Loryma we spent the night.
The wind could be heard howling outside, against the

hills that enclosed our sheltered water as if it were a mountain tarn. Only a fanning ripple touched the centre. The sound of the wind, inarticulate and busy like the world's voice, gave an illusion of safety, of an unassailable peace. If it could penetrate, how many sleeping echoes would it waken? Athenians from Samos, dodging the Dorian Cnidus, picking up ships' tackle at Syme, sheltering at Loryma; Conon, before the battle, with his ninety ships; the Roman fleet that dared not face Hannibal in the offing; Cassius, gathering forces against Rhodes, twenty miles away. Each in their turn passed through the narrow opening and felt the sudden calm. In these places, the natural features have remained unaltered; the moments that visit them, fashioned to one pattern by nature itself, drop like beads on a string, through long pauses, one after the other, into the same silence.

❖   ❖   ❖

We sailed from Cos to Budrum (Halicarnassus). I spent the morning in the castle. Over the deserted walls, on the disused steps, a feeling of intimacy hovered, a touch that once spoke of home to the crusader and could still be recognized.

The goats pushed their hard little worn hooves into places where stones had fallen, and followed the joints of the walls, and cropped the roots that grew in them, and kept the ruins clean. The sea below lay smooth under fanning ripples that moved without breaking its surface. In its transparent depth, in shafts of sun, fish browsed at the castle foundations, investigating them head-on with dull curiosity intent on food. The grass-grown fosse itself seemed like a pool – not free in a universal way as Greek ruins are free, but as if Time had been trapped there, and grown clogged and stagnant, and remained. Nothing of what the castle had been built for counted in it any longer; its language was intelligible to me because it was the language of my people, with few centuries between us; but compared with the idylls of Theocritus, the work of the Knights here was dust.

They too constructed their present, and hacked and destroyed a past to build a dream of such courage that the world of their own age vanished around them, and the world of their promise alone was truly alive. There was no fault in the dream: it was the fosse, the long windowless enclosure, that gave it the feeling of a prison – walls which keep the unbeliever out, which kill Socrates, and confine the spirit whose only home is its immortal freedom.

❖ ❖ ❖

So we too look into our past, treating it as far as we can with respect for its own sake, because of the scattered fragments of truth it must contain. With infinite consideration, with ceaseless care, we disentangle them, and try to keep them intact in their integrity, as free, as far as we can make them, from the twist of our own time and of ourselves – never forgetting that somewhere in that knot is the beginning of a thread that we must follow, on whose right choice the future of all must depend.

❖ ❖ ❖

Who would not be enamoured of Time while he lingers beside us? He is, if one comes to think of it, the closest of all our mortal companions. In his lifelong friendship – capricious, elusive, frightening, delightful – we can remember our youth together and need look forward to no separation except that of death.

❖ ❖ ❖

The word *loyalty* is so black-and-white, so often misapplied, so double-faced and hard to recognize from one side to the other, that perhaps it would be better to leave it altogether out of use? Its presence is assumed, its absence blamed, with a partial and unreasonable passion – rarely the same for him who speaks and him who hears from even the most slightly divergent angle; and the fact is that the word is a collective, whose use with a singular meaning is almost without exception a mistake.

There is always more than one loyalty to be considered. Race, government, custom, origin, religion – one has to choose between them, and the problem is not a simple matter easily dismissed.

❖ ❖ ❖

The great ages pass swiftly – the fifth century in Attica, the fifteenth in Italy, the eighteenth in England. Their ruins last after them longer than they do, with an immobility perhaps equivalent to man's fondness for static laws. But the great age while it lives, when civilization touches its height, moves freely, using its past as if it were alive and not a boundary wall as it becomes in its decline. And there is usually a similarity between such periods – produced by the prosperous middle class that makes them – the bankers, merchants, country gentry, builders and captains of ships. Other more imperial ages may be richer; they may exploit or enjoy what has been nurtured before them; they may spread farther, and – nearly always – last longer: but the secret of life is not in them; the fire they kindle is not their own fire; the settled magnificence of Rome is different in kind from the nature of Greece as she rises, or Florence as she remembers, or England as she builds.

Generalizations, one is told, are dangerous. So is life, for that matter, and it is built up on generalization – from the earliest effort of the adventurer who dared to eat a second berry because the first had not killed him. So I will stick to my generalizing, and hold that the summit of civilization is touched by the middle class. It walks along a razor's edge between the tyrant and the proletariat and is short-lived for that reason.

And, continuing to generalize, I will hold that the

middle class produces civilization because it is the only class constantly trained to come to a conclusion, poised as it is between the depth and height. It is not rich enough to have everything, nor poor enough to have nothing – and has to choose: to choose between a succulent table and a fine library, between travel and a flat in town, between a car and a new baby, or a fur coat and a ball dress: it has enough of the superfluous to give it freedom from necessity, but only through the constant use of discrimination: its life therefore is one long training of the judgement and the will. This by itself need not manufacture greatness; but it is the soil in which it is possible to make it grow. And for this reason, when the rich become too rich and the poor too poor, and fewer and fewer people live under the constant discipline of their decisions, the age of greatness withers. To produce the lifelong stimulus of choice both in thought and action should be the aim of all education, and the statesman ought above all things to provide a government that remains in the hands of people whose life has trained them in the inestimable art of making up their minds.

❖ ❖ ❖

The whole picture of Kekova was spread out in the sunset before us, painted in mortal weakness by poverty and time. It was disturbing and strangely satisfying. Any alleviation, or improvement would have seemed impertinent – a contrast too startling to be borne. For a haunted loveliness was woven into these mean constituents and the dignity it gave them was not to be judged in terms of comfort. The visible world had chosen to build its own perfection out of the short-comings of the human material; and its frailty was not to be counted by success or value, but by this atmosphere of loveliness in which it lingered, beyond the realms of judgement, like the blind loyalties of men.

❖ ❖ ❖

We came close in now. The fjords held rich solitudes of trees that had grown as the soil had fed them, empty of men. The evening scents came to meet us as they had come from the slopes of Caunus, as if incense had been scattered on the air. Beside the last of the Lide promontories we turned into an inlet protected by two wooded islands. A little boat was there in the dusk, in green shadow, watching its nets in the water, whose floating gourds our furrow tilted here and there. Next morning we saw a small hamlet on a ridge: but now, nothing seemed near us but the dark. The trees and water slipped together; the sky ceased to be reflected; the only sound was the splash of our anchor falling. A few landing stones near a ruined hut showed pale in a clearing. Maples and pines had crept up to it, and it had ceased to belong to men. Here *Elfin* rested, like a firefly cosily lighted with our supper cooking inside her, while the darkness pressed upon her, with soft and mothlike wings.   COAST NEAR FETHIYE

❖   ❖   ❖

The water was very deep. It held its light far down inside it like the star in a sapphire: its daily enchantment is never to be forgotten. For what words can give even the ghost of the Aegean bathing? When the body is lost because the radiance and coolness of the world have become a part of it, and nothing seems oneself any longer; and the warmth and light between two darknesses of atmosphere and sea caress all that emerges – the imperceptible moving tide, and our shoulders, and the embracing mountains that burn above us on the noonday edge of their horizon, and in their slower cycle also carry as we do some fire at their heart. There in perfect solitude the pine trees hang over the white rocks and the water lifts us, alive and unresisting, through its own regions, from which a vast loom seems to be weaving sea and earth and sky, out of their basic unity into the varied loveliness of Time. And who can wonder that such hours gave light to the lives that contained them; or who would be mad enough to change them for any money that the world can give? No life is wasted that can remember them, as I hope to do till I have to leave it all.   ST. NICOLAS

❖   ❖   ❖

We were not for underestimating magic – a life-conductor like the sap between the tree-stem and the bark. We know that it keeps dullness out of religion and poetry. It is probable that without it we might die.

Everything in the nature of inspiration belongs to it; and there will be a gloomy world when prophets, artists, and tactful women think they can do without it. The politician and the business man could give it a few moments in their day. For it is easily attainable. It requires a mere suspension of activity – so that the self, in a passive air, may become pure reception, while mystery flowers into an articulate mood with as little interference as possible from the human channel it uses.

This is magic, within reach of us all; a flash where the universe surges up through a creature, who becomes ear, or eye – an unresisting vehicle – void of self, filled and replenished with sights and sounds and feelings that move in and out of perception, so that in his small concreteness, according to his capacity and abnegation, the roots of being may grow. This is what the egocentric loses, and substitutes for it his miserable person. And perhaps magic alone is the cause of the happiness of primitive and true country people, for whom all pleasures of sophistication are compensated, if they only knew it, by this awareness.

◆   ◆   ❖

The life of insecurity is the nomad's achievement. He does not try, like our building world, to believe in a stability which is non-existent; and in his constant movement with the seasons, in the lightness of his hold, puts something right, about which we are constantly wrong. His is in fact the reality, to which the most solid of our structures are illusion; and the ramshackle tents in their crooked gaiety, with cooking-pots propped up before them and animals about, show what a current flows round all the stone erections of the ages. The finest ruin need only be lamented with moderation, since its living essence long ago entered the common stream. No thought of this kind is likely to come into the head of the Turkish Yürük (though it could be familiar to the imagination of the Arab); they are happy to shelter their goats in the warmth or the shade that they find, whether the ruins be of Nineveh or Rome. In Limyra they were partly settled and partly arriving from the mountains, with long trains of camels and flocks, and horses straying loosely on the wandering track. Their women invited us, where the tents and pillows were stacked in order; they were cheerful and fierce, unlike the peasant, and dressed in brighter colours – equals of their men or of anyone, as one may be if one lives under the hardness of necessity and makes insecurity one's refuge.

❖   ❖   ❖

I wondered, as I have so often done in Arabia, at the *aristocracy* of them all – that lean and vital quality shared by the nomad creatures – the thin Saluki dogs, the horses and goats hungry and free, the shepherd-girl's little triangular face and Mona Lisa lips, the wide-awake eyes of the lads and easy equal manners, meeting their life as it comes – the loveliness of even the old women at the well.

It is easy for the peasant, and for all of us who live in civilization and think to make the world more habitable, to point out that the nomad does very little. He leaves things as he finds them, destroying them in a small way if it suits him. He does not spend his life as we do in altering the accidents that happen to us so as to make them more bearable – but he accepts them with gaiety and endures them with fortitude, and this is his triumph and his charm.

We may think reasonably enough that we dominate circumstances more than he does, since we adapt them to our
needs: but he has discovered that the meaning of life is
more important than its circumstance – and this freedom
of the soul, in which all things that happen come and go,
makes him splendid – him and his gaunt women and dogs
and horses, on the edge of starvation in the rain and
the sun.

His life does not allow him to forget the greater size of
the world; and no amount of civilization is worth the loss
of this fundamental sense of proportion between the
universe and man.

⬦   ⬦   ⬦

The Stoic ages have never completely left us. They
turned from the external universe and questioned the
human soul inwardly, for such contentment as it requires,
and did what they could to loosen its mortal attachments.
And it is ever a twilight world that abstains or refuses.
The Ionian dawn was lost, and the bars of the cage pressed
in; until a later teaching surmounted the barrier, and
stretched the world out again into its unfenced frame.
Happiness, as I rode down towards the beach in the
evening, seemed to me to belong to those three ages, ever
with a growing awareness: to the nomad, whose infinity
lies about him unquestioned; to the Aegean sailing without fear towards a yet undiscovered horizon; and to those,
in the religions of our time, 'whose service is perfect
freedom' since they have seen their bars melted and
infinity renewed. Freedom is the secret. They can accept
the cage of this world because it does not really exist,
and they live in their liberty beyond it – with a delight
different in its accent from the Stoic's endurance.

⬦   ⬦   ⬦

When Mehmet had given us our supper in the cabin of
Elfin, we climbed into the dinghy and rowed about the

southern harbour under the full moon. Three of the three
hundred fishing caiques of Budrum were there beside us,
the day's catch of sponges spread out on the cut stone
quay-side of Triopium. The boats themselves squatted dark
in the headland shadow, their rough and tattered sailors
all asleep. A haunted, a magical remoteness lay on the
sleeping town; the tiers of its streets, the great con-
glomerate blocks of its foundations still looked in the night
like darkened gold; the grey wall of the high skyline and
the hill-side it was cut from melted, as if into their element,
unseen into the sky. Only the water was awake, motionless but filled with shafts of moonlight – a warm yellow
light that sank through layer upon layer, through depth
upon depth to reach and gild the sand. These shafts of
light, fluid in the mystery around them, seemed to me like
the days of Cnidus – the few known, the infinite number
unknown.

As we drifted, looking for the mole, the moonlight under
water crossed like swords, like wavering veils, like phan-
toms – like all the events and dreams: and suddenly, with
a strange emotion, we saw very far down yet clear in the
moonlit depth the pavement of the mole's foundations, a
broad causeway of blocks gnawed by the sea for more than
two thousand years, laid there with pride and toil when
the Cnidians still trusted their freedom and the city was
young.

⋄   ⋄   ⋄

It is a pity perhaps that we chiefly study a classical age
which we do not look like imitating, rather than the
Hellenistic and the Greco-Roman, full of examples and
warnings: for they were working through wars, through
revolutions, federations and monarchies, towards unity.
However imperfectly attained and uncertain in its harmony, this was their step in history. Innumerable partic-
ularisms comparable to modern nationalisms impeded; the
great powers, with Helots in Laconia, with cleruchies on
the islands, threw dark shadows; the continuation of small

autonomies retarded the whole process. These hindrances made the Greek world uncertain and out of time: they brought to an end a great age which could only have continued if a perception of unity had prevailed and transformed it.

The notion flashed by with Alexander like a wing in the sun. It showed, as it passed, how the capacity for greatness persists; and as it faded in darkness, it left behind it in the barbarian night – like a touchstone, or Cinderella slipper on the steps of the Greek palace – the civilization by which we live today.

❖   ❖   ❖

In my childhood, I have lain so for hours, peering from a boulder into the pool of a Dartmoor stream, which the current had missed. There its life went on, in a filtered light, a subtle brilliant obscurity, surrounded by stillness like a mirror – close but unapproachable, so that the roots or the stones I leaned on became divided into two separated selves, by the thin elemental line of water – the present and the past, and yet the same. . . .

Such was Phaselis, solitary and almost forgotten in its pool. The brightness of the Aegean filled its three harbours, and the current once ran here; and the stream of all our world poured briefly through with the troops of Alexander. What brought him to so remote a province, and kept him among its hills while the armies of Darius were strengthening in the East? A few stray words are all the help we have – the talk with Parmenio at Miletus, the disbanding of the navy, the omen of the eagle that foretold a conquest of the sea-ways from the shore. It is the gleam of a fin, a movement among brown shadows in the pool; but the long thoughts that preceded the decisions, the influences of envoys and their persuasions, their very existences, have sunk indistinguishable into the settled dark.

❖   ❖   ❖

When we visited Phaselis again another year, we discovered that the hamlet of Tekrova is just in sight behind it; the woodcutters had been among the ruins; and the enchantment was broken. But we had seen it haunted. For one day, with the evening and the morning that followed, the shadows of the pines ran freely through the street and in the rooms of the ruined houses; the temple columns were as warm to the darting lizards as ever they had been to the hands of the devout who leaned against them; and amid the solitary rustlings – the breaking of a twig, a breath in the grasses, a ripple suddenly splashing on the sand – one could hear the voices of the dead city with their gaiety insubstantial and diminished, fading, elusive, like Eurydice, into the arms of night.

Alexander's Path

Asia Minor 1956

In this solitude not even the goatherd was about, though his flock was browsing. But it was a fortunate day, and a soldier overtook us just as we reached the top of the ascent. He came up from Demre, as he had been doing two thousand years ago, to 'keep watch over the sea'; and he told me that I would find more ruins if I walked towards the headland. . . . Even now, if I think of that view on some winter's day, the freedom and the light return, the glistening solitude possesses me; the Aegean is plumb below, darkened with sunlight, where vagrant islands dance unfrequented and the morning landscape curves by itself alone.

I sat there idly, and far away the coast of Demre spread waves on flat sands in easy patterns. Like speech or writing they pressed with ceaseless variety from their sea, and under the lightness and foam their run was short or longer according to the depth from which they came.

NEAR DEMRE

❖   ❖   ❖

Alexander at the age of twenty-two came to Asia, and the plan of hellenizing the world he brought from his background, his youth, his teachers, and – possibly most of all – his father. He transformed the plan, but the essence of it was there already: he seized and developed the impulse of his time. The training of youth, instituted in Athens about 335 B.C. and derived from Plato's Laws, spread through the Greek world and into barbarian lands; Alexander's games and competitions in Asia, literary and athletic, developed into festivals held for generations in his honour; and theatres in cities soon began to be built in stone. When the Romans came, a vast network, not pure in race but deeply Greek in feeling, had spread from the Mediterranean to India, and the hellenizing that passed into the Roman world has lived to this day. One may remember the dream of Pyrrhus before his march, when he thought Alexander called to him and offered to assist him. But Alexander lay ill and Pyrrhus asked how he could do it. 'I will do it,' said he, 'with my name': and his name has done it to our time.

Even if this were all, it would be a record of conquest no other human being has attained before or after. But it is not all. The first part of his plan was in the fashion of his day and of his people, but the second was shared neither by his teachers nor by his friends. It was his own, and it steeped him in loneliness. More than two thousand years have had to pass, and Alexander's dream of a united world is still a dream: it has waited, like a sound in mountain walls, for the centuries to give an echo back, and has found a common voice at last and echoes in many hearts. What would one not give to know how it first began?

As I sat in the stillness of the theatre of Oenoanda, where the spirit of Greece lived though probably no Greek had built it, I began to think of what can happen to change a lad of twenty-two who comes for the first time to Asia. Romance reaches the romantic – and Alexander was passionately romantic; and human sympathies come to the warm-hearted, and the Alexander saga could never have existed if his heart had not been warm. Time too must be remembered – the fact that a year and a half or more was spent along the coast of Asia Minor before ever the battle of Issus was fought; and five years before he first adopted the Persian dress in Parthia.

Aristander, his friend and intimate adviser from childhood, was a Lycian; and when they came to Aristander's people on this coastland, it was with friendship and protection of a Carian queen behind them. These nations were all half hellenized already, so that it was no very sudden step from Europe into Asia; the difficulty of language – the main barrier since Babel – was here largely overcome. And even if this had not been so, I thought of all the Englishmen who have written, and looked with the eyes of youth on these lands and been enchanted, and how the division of customs has melted and the human bond asserting itself remains. This surely happened; and one can watch the change, from the confident young victor who sent, from the Granicus, the spoils of the barbarians, to the man who comforted the mother of Darius whom he had unknowingly offended.

✧ ✧ ✧

The reticences of the living are generally greater than those of the dead. The element of fear is in them; and the happy intimacy, the recognition of one spirit with another, is not so frequent as it might be in this world. But to the scholar, who seeks for no response, but only to listen, the barriers of time are open; the fragments that come drifting through them are warm with life.

✧ ✧ ✧

It took us two and a half instead of one and a half hours to reach Alanya because the jeep's whole footboard, with its brake, jerked up at intervals towards the driver. Mustapha finally took a screw from somewhere else and screwed it down, with unimpaired good temper; in spite of all the things that happen to their cars I have never heard a driver in Asia use an impatient word to a machine. Watching while the rain splashed him with a halo, I wondered, for the thousandth time, whether it is better to be resourceful, or to do away with the necessity for resource and replace a screw in time. This great question may involve the future of our species; but luckily I need not decide it.

✧ ✧ ✧

Now that I had escaped from the squalor of inns into these country places, I never lay down to rest without a thought of gratitude and wonder for the goodness of the Turkish peasants as I found them. The Arabs and Greeks have more aristocratic virtues that lead to enterprise and hatreds and adventures based on exclusion. Goodness, since it is based on sharing, can never be aristocratic, and the Turkish villagers in their poverty are ready to share with all. The simplicity of their goodness is touching – its anxiety to help, its honourableness and active kindness, its love for children and flowers. Unlike most of the world, they do not undervalue their own – but show ready pleasure if any poor possession, air, view, or water, or any attractiveness in the hard and simple life is praised. They turn willingly from all their own distresses, delighted with whatever the humble excellence may be. Nor can I remember, during all my three visits to Turkey, to have been offended by a discourteous word.

❧   ❧   ❧

In early spring the bay of Antalya lies under a mist slightly raised above the surface of the water and filled with sunlight, until the warmth of day sucks it up. I would watch it from a slanting little breakfast shop that overhangs the harbour. The six tiled domes of the Seljuk mosque, now the museum, are there in the foreground with a minaret like a bunch of asparagus beside them, rosy as if its bricks had been scrubbed – which indeed they had been, by the Department of Antiquities which has repaired them. Beyond these, brown roofs and the tops of trees push out from hidden gardens; and beyond them a caique might have been moving out from Antalya with the dawn: she would leave a curved trail, marked by the current, as wavering and edgeless as the seasonal pathways made by the feet of flocks; and beyond her and the misty bay, the Chelidonian peninsula spread its tented blue festoons from peak to peak. Every shade of azure was caught by those pinnacles and in those valleys, and their height seemed to vary with the hours, from its morning simplicity to the magnificence of sunset, when only outlines showed and their shadows were thrown across the sea. Or perhaps most beautiful when the full moon hung over Cyprus invisible in the south; then the foreground roofs became velvety and obscure like scabious flowers, the walls and towers that remain were arched over dark eclipses; and the far mountains rose into light as if the heavens above them opened and their earth were winged.

⬥   ⬥   ⬥

These serene wide hills, pale and striped evenly with snow; these waters in shallow temporary lakes with grassy strips of islands; cattle in droves about purposeless rivers, where all seems to move slowly in uncrowded spaces and oxen drag the solid wooden wheels invented far away for the steppes of Asia; this glitter of the self-sufficing air above the jade-green velvet pale barley and the corn, and brilliance of wild almond saplings coloured like the shining lichen of the rocks; this vivid late spring of English flowers – drifts of vetch purple and yellow, grey-leaved cerastium, cornflower and anchusa and mullein, white roses and the orange-red bushy poppy of the plateau – all open suddenly above the bent shoulders of the valleys as one breaks upon the Anatolian plain.

⬥   ⬥   ⬥

In the rapture of such beauty one could scarcely have borne a companion. One looked not at but *through* experience, as if life in general were a window to interpret the world, and this must be perhaps a solitary pastime, the secret of travel. The stray road-side events are a part of its solitude; but companionship – unless with one 'more me than I am myself' – produces the destructive shock which every artist knows.

⬥   ⬥   ⬥

Whenever a mare came near the road, my pony woke up from his boredom and arched his neck and turned into a thin brown flame between my knees. The bond is very strong. From beyond our sight, animal or human, the physical spark lights the world's interest and beauty – a transformation whence all our arts and pride derive; and thinking with horror of the gelding of creatures – as if mere living were everything that mattered – I was pleased to manage my horse's difficult little curvets about the road. A young friend's complaint came into my mind: she told me that dancing is no pleasure, since too many young men are too much interested in men; and I thought of long-ago dances – the magic when the arms that held one were the right arms, the dullness when they were not – and the poverty of a life that misses – not sentiment, not affection, not friendship, for these can be enjoyed in many versions – but that ripple which runs like the wind over a harp from behind the beginning of time.

✦   ✧   ✧

To Mehmet the Jeep – reduced to a skeleton, patient and prehistoric under the trees, and surrounded by screws – was not a mere machine and a rather unattractive one at that. It was El Dorado, his dream. It was La Princesse Lointaine and the New Age all in one, to which the 'pick-up' that played ten tunes by itself belonged. Nor had he stinted or neglected anything about it, for the Turkish cars that can get no spares because of the present restrictions need a great deal of resourcefulness in their service.

One is always grateful for the sight of pure, harmless, and undiluted happiness in this world: and that is what Mehmet enjoyed, sailing up and down with his Jeep well dusted on the road between Antalya and Elmali, and greeted along it all the way: and it was not money-mindedness but simply easy kindness that had brought him over this gruelling pass.

✧   ✧   ✦

Nothing could get Mehmet and his Jeep to move. 'You are tired ,'said he; 'so am I'; and the Jeep was *bozulmush* when I was packed and ready – an ominous word whose full implications I was to learn in the next few days. Mehmet, with that endearing blue-eyed air of a classical demigod who has accidentally hit middle age, maddened me with frustration, and the strain of not knowing the language well enough to be effectively annoyed. It would anyway have been of no use. The art of travel, and perhaps of life, is to know when to give way and when not to, and it is only after the level of grievances has risen so as to be obvious to all that a scene does any good. The moment came, however. Scattering grammar to right and left, I made a speech, and Mehmet tore himself from the arms of his family and started. The Jeep, said he, was in order; we left Elmali while the beautiful Ottoman mosque was calling its faithful at dawn.

❖   ❖   ❖

A good traveller does not much mind the uninteresting places. He is there to be inside them, as a thread is inside the necklace it strings. The world, with unknown and unexpected variety, is a part of his own Leisure; and this living participation is, I think, what separates the traveller and the tourist, who remains separate, as if he were at a theatre, and not himself a part of whatever the show may be.

A certain amount of trouble is required before one can enter into such unity, since every country, and every society inside it, has developed its own ritual of living, as well as its own language. Some knowledge of both is essential, and – just as our circumambient air contains melody but cannot express it until a voice is given – so a technique or voice is needed for human, or indeed for all intercourse. To find this unity makes me happy: its discovery comes unexpectedly upon me, not only with people, but with animals, or trees or rocks, or days and nights in their mere progress. A sudden childish delight envelops me and the frontiers of myself disappear.

❖   ❖   ❖

The femininity of the Levant is kept indoors there, but only to be more fit for pleasure; its clothes and easy contours are made to go to bed with, and the women, when this age is over, think no longer of their appearance and

183

do not, in fact, try to please in any other way. But while their tide is with them, the young women's veiling is royal; protected like idols, they breathe security and move with enviable safety in a walled world, with anything but submission in their seclusion. They are set apart, yet they remain individual and are not destroyed. But the Turks have a middle-class Victorian attitude to their harim and expect it to be there to serve them, with a constant feeling that women are not complete entities in themselves. The peasants make them work more heavily than they do in Arabia, and civilization which requires feminine time and attention, seems to suffer and decline where women work very hard. Yet even here the home feeling is pleasant after the dingy world of men. And especially so since the Turk – in spite of his strength and self-reliance – is dull. He is as different from the Arab as anyone can be, even physically, with his good head, neither long nor broad but sanely balanced, and capable safe hands and general regularity of feature, compared to the long beduin hands and swinging movements and faces furrowed with emotions that belong to the nomad lands, at any rate, of Arabia.

Unlike the Arab, who cares for nothing else, the Turk is not interested in the abstract. The abstract, that interprets the world and makes it no longer impenetrable and impervious, and is reached by curiosity one step beyond our borders, means nothing to him. The Arab, with his tiresomeness, is an artist. To him the unknown world *is real*.

And women and artists, wherever they may be, are always pushed a little way over that abstract edge, since the two ends of life – the greatest and the smallest – are in their hands. The unknown exists for them and, for this reason, the woman's side of the house was always an indescribable improvement on the dreariness of the man-made hotel.

◇   ◇   ◇

Women are handicapped in Turkey by their unimportance, which is so absolute that even flattery is disregarded; the familiar expedient of making men feel better and cleverer than they are fails, since female praise is too idle to count.

⊰ ⊰ ⊰

I spent the afternoon resting, until the horse came for a gentle ride round the cliff-walls, where the tombs climb one above the other with a busy feeling as if they were a street of shops. Goatherd children with charming manners scrambled with me up steps nearly effaced. They refused my few pence, and asked with mysterious interest for the figures of the population of Britain. What they learnt at school I never discovered (I have never discovered what I have learnt myself) except that they are taught to think of the red flag of Turkey as a flower that grows like the poppy, out of the heart of their soil; and their beautiful good manners they learn at home.

My guide, though living so near, had never himself been up to the cliffs. A party drinking tea under an almond tree would have come with us, if they had not been celebrating the father's death like the figures reclined and feasting in the tombs above. From those carved porches we looked at the gorge of Demre, whose wheatfields filled the flat that once was sea. The scar of the defile above was dark in shadow, but all else glowed uncontaminated and fine in the late light, as if it were molten gold. The authorities of the townlet, police and müdür, were strolling by a path where the wall of the old enclosure of St. Nicholas still shows though all except the church has been demolished. They bowed and hoped I was happy. A woman carrying cucumbers from her fields gave a gift from the bundle to the stranger. And even a poor bitch, suckling her four puppies by the road-side, looked up transfigured in that peaceful glow: she lifted her careful gentle eyes towards us, as if their ceaseless awareness of darkness and danger were slipped for a moment into its sheath.

⊰ ⊰ ⊰

Below Sagalassus in the plain, the spring had come; we looked down on cultivated hollows like spoons among the hills where the shallow lakes of winter were drying; there the poplars shimmered as if with sequins on silver, the walnuts curled infant leaves bright and brown as polished leather, the pear trees were thick and tight with blossoms like Victorian nosegays in every sheltered hollow. People were out, riding or walking near the villages; the manes and tails of grazing horses were ruffled in the breeze; women were weeding, kneeling in rows; or hoeing, one behind the other, with a man at ease to direct them; and oxen were ploughing, four or five teams together. All were in groups, spaced here and there like a ballet of the works of spring.

❖　❖　❖

Bairam was beginning. Among the calls of the muezzin at their appointed hours the end of Ramadhan was announced with blasts of sirens. Electric lights sprang up round the minarets in a primrose dusk where swifts, or perhaps swallows, were darting. And a vague buzz of pleasure filled the air.

I walked about my terrace quietly contented, as if the world and I belonged to each other far from all personal tensions – the feeling of a haven; and as I watched the swallows I thought of my private unhappiness, so long ago – nearly forty years –; how deep it had been, and how it had healed, and all had turned to life; as if, in the agony of one's heart, one were kneaded into a substance subtle enough to melt into existence, and could see one's own soul, and everyone's for that matter, stepping out small and brave under the tall illuminated archway of its past.

ANTALYA

❖　❖　❖

Between the town and the river, where Alexander camped within the outer wall among the little houses, the

186

theatre stands on flat ground, like a box from which the lid has been lifted. Proud, limited, and magnificent, there is a prison air about it – a difference as of death and life that one feels between the Roman and the Greek. No landscape stretches here beyond a low and unobtrusive stage, for the easy coming and going of the gods. Human experience, that moved with freedom and mystery, is here walled in with balconies and columns; its pure transparency, the far horizon window, is lost.

In the Greek theatre, with its simple three-doored stage and chorus undertone of sorrow, the drama of life could penetrate, without any barrier between them, the surrounding vastness of the dark. ASPENDUS

❖   ❖   ❖

The people of the Middle East (who are the only people beyond Europe that I know) think that an external discipline is sufficient to reproduce a way of life which they admire, and which strangely enough happens to be ours. Now this is not a thing that can be handed over or imitated. It cannot be done. No living organism can be copied; for a civilization is not made by mere acts, but by the traditions and impulses behind them. These alone can be handed on, to be assimilated, nurtured, and reborn in a new shape, alive and different in new hands. Unless such a process takes place the mere imitation is dead.

The invaders of the Greek and Roman world too copied, and we call their labour decadence, and wonder at the chasm that divides it from its lovely inspiration. Their clumsy efforts were mere effigies; the true descent was evolved slowly from some assimilation that fashioned it in centuries of Seljuk or Byzantine, or in far Norman cathedrals that have lost even the memory of when they came. Because this hidden process is so sorrowful, we rightly hesitate to press our western pattern, or try to plait it in sparingly, so as not to destroy other strands which

187

may be good. Nor do we feel sure that what we offer is better than what the imitators lose.

⋄   ⋄   ⋄

Large tombs with long inscriptions stood carved in hellenized barbarian smugness, as if the bourgeois spirit, preoccupied with other men's opinions, must carry its burden of responsibility even through the forgetfulness of Time. For it was as if Time itself, like a tide withdrawing, had receded from this high lip of the valley and no whisper of its movement were any longer heard.

⋄   ⋄   ⋄

Most of this, except the *heraion*, seemed late; there was a slickness about it, as if the architect, after too much building, no longer respected each work separately for itself, but copied merely. That is decadence, I thought, as I wandered among the thorns – in architecture, in life, and in literature also. As the architect his stone, so the writer too keeps his idea side by side in his mind with the sentences that describe it, to see them continually together, so that reality may rule his words, in a human proportion, and the fact and its reporting may not deviate one from the other and truth be lost. Decadence is their divergence, a gap between the conception and its expression, a slackening of the discipline that unites us with vision: and excellence, which alone matters in a world that neglects it, lies almost entirely in this coincidence of the thing with its expression. However humble or unimportant the object may be, this is true, and even the bows and ribbons of la Pompadour are remembered because they were *right*.

ARIASSUS

⋄   ⋄   ⋄

The happy side of Alanya belongs to the beauty of Alaeddin's city, which gives it its stamp and outlives all the other ages – ancient, Ottoman, or Crusading – that encrust the fortified pyramid on its hill. Beyond all military architectures, the early Greek and the Seljuk seem to me to express the delight of their building. Functional as they are – for they allow no unessential to mislead them – they refuse to be limited to economic terms: they reach their perfection regardless of expense or effort, and a sort of radiance inevitably follows, as if the axle of immortality ran through them. An absence of triviality, a depth and fearlessness triumphant over fashion is reached by all such works – the Greek wall, the Seljuk tower, the wing of the jet fighter, and all the inventions that grasp life so neatly and joyfully that death ceases to matter in the count.

⋄   ⋄   ⋄

When Alexander and his friends walked here, the citadels were intact on their hills. Their walls and towers were in sight from one to the other, with broader fields about them than now. Some pillared temple or portico must always have been appearing, with the snows of Ak Dagh western or eastern behind it, as one rode past the lion-headed sarcophagi to the straight gateways across the ridge's undulations, along a road where the sea was out of sight but always felt. It ran like a backbone through the level landscape, painted like some medieval missal with spiky ridges and small clear points of rock surrounding flats of corn, where the army rested beside the scanty waters that still remain.

It was easy in our own slow travel to picture the comradeship the day's march produces, with stray discomforts and sudden good moments of shade or water, or scent of honeysuckle blown across the track; or to think how the king's sayings were handed from mouth to mouth along the column, while he walked under his broad shallow hat of the Macedonian fashion at its head. The boyhood friendships, continued through these marches, lasted him all his life, and the injury to his memory and to his family, when it came, came through the absent Cassander, who had no share in these enchanted days.

189

The stories trickle haphazard into history, mostly from a later time, for of this march in Anatolia hardly a detail has come down. But the character is always the same, ardent, courteous, and impetuous, with a certainty that never hesitated to strike when it was essential, and a willingness to spare when it could.

'Bear it,' he said, as a soldier passed fainting under a load of gold which he had taken from his exhausted mule and was trying to carry. 'You need only reach your tent, to keep it for yourself.'

In our day, Wavell, in the desert mess of the Eighth Army, would send for a double Scotch and leave it, so that the stewards when he went away might have a drink which only an officer could order.

❖   ❖   ❖

Solitude floated up from the vertical gorges, filled with cypress or cedar as if with black spears. The silence buried the sound of its own waters, and a thin haze, spun in the blueness of air, divided one range from another, as if the heights wore haloes. The trees closed in above us, and below – juniper, with soft fresh needles; and the harder aromatic cypress; maples, with their younger leaves light against the green in damp places; carob, and Judas, some sort of rhus with round leaves and feathery purple plumes, and the red boughs of the arbutus like sudden naked arms. Higher up, the oak leaves lifted into sunlight, and their trunks, and those of a tall tree like a chestnut, stood furrowed like stone among the strange hieratic stones. These ribs of rock, symmetrically ranked, descended, one felt, into the hill's foundations, and the bare rain-washed scaffolding that shows must be a part of the hidden scaffolding of earth.

❖   ❖   ❖

The hill-side, warm and silent under filmy cloud like milk that the sun was drinking, seemed alive not with life but with time.

❖   ❖   ❖

I slept in the doctor's house in comfort, above a slope of cornfields soft as water, where the sound of water ran too, sinuous and long as a snake's backbone that slides from vertebra to vertebra, in a subtle incarnation of repose.

❖   ❖   ❖

'If you think it better,' said Mehmet, so unselfishly 'I, will get you a good new jeep, and you will still be able to drive round by the Marsyas gorges and reach Chivril (near the source of the Maeander) before night.'

My detour seemed to be widening to embrace the whole of western Turkey. I knew the twisting road of the Marsyas gorges, and the thought of Mehmet at every corner was too much. I accepted his offer, and with the eastern promptness so surprising when it comes, a jeep was found. My luggage was transferred; Mehmet appeared with apples and bread and cherries; finances were sorted out, and a present given to Mahmud who took every small kindness as if it were an opening into paradise; and the moment came to say good-bye. Suddenly and surprisingly we were none of us able to say anything, but shook hands with eyes full of tears. The new driver settled in his seat, and bowed towards me. 'May your journey be happy,' said he. 'If Allah wills,' said I, and we went.

For hours, as the day wore on and we sped with a wonderfully pleasant nimbleness round the corners of the twisted valley, this departure distressed me. Everything I had done had been wrong. I knew from years of experience that one should never have an appointment at the other end when one travels in Asia. And even after this mistake, I could have sent a few telegrams and borne the heat, and waited till the Jeep and my foot recovered in Fethiye. It was not my fault, perhaps, but I could have avoided all the trouble by not hurrying.

I *had* hurried, and the whole tenor of my companions' life was disrupted – so vulnerable to an outer world is their system, which pleased and contented them, and allowed

191

them to practise their virtues. The poor Jeep, their pride, had been shown up for what it was, gimcrack and unreliable; and they were left in a strange part of the country, to get back as best they could over all those mountains alone. The vision of the two figures, crouching in the dust and serving their idol with spanners, came to me at intervals and brought tears every time. It must be fatigue, I thought, not having eaten since two in the morning; and I took one of Mehmet's apples; but the tears continued. It *is* my fault, I thought. What happens to people because of their dealings with us *must* be our business. It is brotherhood, the best thing we find in Asia – brotherhood not because people are the same but because they are different. It is a monstrous wish to make people equal before you can think of them as brothers: the other is the real democracy, and we find and spoil it.

One's sympathy, I reflected, is nearly always tinged with exasperation in the 'old world' of Asia: because it is outside our philosophy, doomed to failure in an incompatible world in which it is inefficient and hopelessly outchanced. But it is always resilient under the troubles it has asked for; free of envy, and with no thought that one human being is better than any other because of money, or of any human possession other than goodness and good manners. And to come upon a code like that and help to destroy it is cause enough for sorrow.

Riding to the Tigris

1958

It was many years since I had spent a night among the tents; the sight of them, seventy or so in the hollow of the mountain, filled me as it always does with delight and pity; for they seem to me to show what our houses forget or disguise – a security based not on strength but on fragility, at rest on the surface of the world like a seagull on a wave.

⋄   ⋄   ⋄

As the day waned, we seemed to be entering a prison between the beetling crags. Their summits led towards what looked like gulfs of a dark conflagration, because of the flame-like soaring outlines of the rock. Satanic was the word. I hunted for it and found it, thinking that no living flame but some such stationary fire long petrified and dead, with no alteration within it but decay, can alone picture the immobility of Hell. The sun by day and the moon by night travel here far away, not unseen but sterile, and the stars can get no answer from dead heights. Ruin alone seemed to depend from those tiered buttresses untouched by vegetation. The sides of the great gorges of Euphrates that run towards Erzinjan are polished like the pillars of a temple, but here the masses of the mountains crumble away in pleats of shale and lie at the feet of all their precipices as baseless, shifting, and nameless as sand.

GREAT ZAB GEORGE

⋄   ⋄   ⋄

The flocks move from morning to evening in their migrations, with one shepherd ahead of them and one behind them, under the clinging discomfort of their own dust. The dust creeps about the landscape above them, to the height of a man's eyes, and reddens and weighs down their curled fleeces; and the sheep, plodding through the ages, nose the ground and bury their eyes each in the coat of the one before it, kicking up their own troubles from their own soil, patient, unquestioning, and like mankind resolute to hide their faces from the goal of their marching, trusting to a shepherd that only their leader can see.

⬦   ⬦   ⬦

The road-makers had a small camp of white tents in a hollow, and here the engineer was relaxing in the obvious belief that the labours of his day were over, when I reminded him that it was not in the middle of emptiness in the hands of the foreman from Erzerum that I was to be deposited, but in the tents of the Mayor of Beiteshebab in his *yaila*. Accounts in Hakkiari had varied as to the distance of these tents, making them anything between half an hour's walk and a day's ride; and I had expected and now discovered the longer distance to be the right one.

The engineer, tied to a road as if it were his umbilical cord, looked round the vast ranges of hills now tremblingly aetherial in the midday sun. A Pegasus, he seemed to think, might break out of the landscape. But nothing was in sight except flocks of sheep and goats, whose spacing on various slopes made the distances vaster and the loneliness more secure. The goats were scattered in dots, the sheep strung in lines like trails of streptococci, and the two together, the white and the black, made a sort of musical notation among the rocks. I sat contemplating it in a pleasant peace, comfortably provided with a mattress, delighted to have reached the end of the road, and sure that something useful would happen fairly soon, since no one would want to have me on their hands without a tent to sleep in.

⬦   ⬦   ⬦

I was sorry for him, still damp from the egg with youth, and so anxious to be grand. While we had squatted comfortably with shepherd boys on the ground, drinking their *yaourt*, he had stood, refusing the half of my Burberry and eventually preferring a little patch of waterlogged earth

196

of his own. He was not unfriendly, but anxious about his
dignity, and that takes all one's time when sitting on one's
luggage on a mule. But now we had been out for five
hours; the sun had been shining upon us down the shade-
less slopes, and without a hat and with his thin shoes and
his civilized clothes, and a headache, and the violin case
in his hand, he had watched me ride under my parasol
on my clever little pony while Abdullah dismounted and
walked the laden mule. I had offered to tie the violin in
with my bedding, but he clung to it, 'for it is what I shall
please myself with in my solitary evenings during the next
few years'; and he had rejected my suggestion that a
handkerchief, wetted and knotted, might keep the sun
off and relieve his head. In a burst of confidence, he had
told me of his home, and of his training in the teachers'
college, and – looking at the forbidding ranges that piled
themselves between him and his memories more solidly
with every passing hour – had said that he had thought
in a year or so to marry, 'but how could I bring a wife
here, into this savage land?'

◇   ◇   ◇

The intimacy of the open air united us in silence.

As I rode along I began to wonder at this word and
what it means; truthfulness above all things, the relative
truthfulness, at all events, of one person responding to that
of another, without which there can be no friendship,
marriage, or good human relationship at all. And after
that, so as to become possible, intimacy must be articulate
– not necessarily in language, but by some medium which
both can understand. Now Abdullah and I could not
communicate very much, because his Turkish did not yet
come naturally to him, but we both belonged to the open
air and were at home in the hills, and not many words
were needed between us. But the young teacher, whether
he talked with either of us or remained silent, was just as
much a stranger as ever, for he had been too overlaid
with education to be truthful for a moment even with

197

himself. It would take years of experience, I reflected, for Psyche to work herself out of that cocoon.

⋄ ⋄ ⋄

The actual stature of man is no greater now than it was near his beginning: he is made tall only by standing on the heap of his ages, and using his past.

⋄ ⋄ ⋄

One of the basic differences between the English and the Eastern Mediterranean is their attitude to clothes, and I think one might clear up a serious little pocket of ignorance if one could make the substance of this difference quite plain. The whole difficulty is that the English attitude is one of *place*, while the Mediterranean in general and the eastern part of it in particular look upon clothes as a visible expression of *status*; we dress for *where* we are, irrespective of status, and the Turks for *what* they are, irrespective of place.

⋄ ⋄ ⋄

I was happy to be out in the wild and open world, with night and the long-unaccustomed slight spice of danger. Darkness fell at six-thirty, but the moon rose behind us, and trees and shrubs, distorted into strange sub-human shapes in the twilight, swam clear out into loveliness, as if their earth had crumbled into gold.

⋄ ⋄ ⋄

I flew on a long way home from Istanbul to Baghdad, and looked before sunrise across the Tigris lands, towards the Hakkiari mountains from the west. They were awakening and uncoiling far below. Beneath an orange rim their amethyst veils were shot with flashing tremors, as if spears of light were wounding the recesses; and cloud cumuli, folded like shells and green-white like the petal-spring of lilies, stood round the eastern bay. The sky there was sharp and clear, and fortress bastions floated in its distance, sheer and unscalable rectangles of cloud.

All this began to disintegrate and move, with mists wrapping and unwrapping above the scrambled ranges; and from their chaos Tigris and the Western Khabur, that flows down to Euphrates, coiled out towards the sun. Already, in the cloister-light of dawn they flashed their mirrors, and wandered apart, one to the sleeping desert, the other to its gorges out of sight. There was no green in the chaos below, but nests of rock, and eel-like writhing ranges with sharp edges, where one could feel the plastic fingers of wind and water working on the substances of earth till rock alone remains.

❖   ❖   ❖

I began to wonder again why I, and so many others like me, should find ourselves in these recondite places. We like our life intensified perhaps. Travel does what good novelists also do to the life of every day, placing it like a picture in a frame or a gem in its setting, so that the intrinsic qualities are made more clear. Travel does this with the very stuff that everyday life is made of, giving to it the sharp contour and meaning of art: and unless it succeeds in doing this, its effect on the human being is not, I believe, very great. To the deeply imaginative, no doubt architecture, painting or music, and to the less adventurous the art of fiction are sufficient strengtheners and discriminators – and most people anyway try to avoid having their feelings intensified: for indeed one must be strong to place oneself alone against the impact of the unknown world.

❖   ❖   ❖

Far too agitated to continue the evening conversation in the porch, I took refuge with the Commandant and his wife, and went to bed as soon as I had eaten . . . exhausted, chiefly by emotion; and I now lay in my bed and never slept. Anger poured over me in waves as if it were the

199

hot tide of a sea. It was not in me: it was outside, and it overwhelmed me. The monstrosity of bureaucracy, I thought: always the pint-pot judging the gallon, the scribe's, the door-keeper's world. Always the stupidity of people who feel certain about things they never try to find out. A world that *educates* people to be ignorant – that is what this world of ours is. . . .

With a nostalgia that hurt like a pain I thought of England; perhaps it was the singing of the waters in the night that brought her so poignantly before me. But it was of her people that I thought: a modest people, where this terrible nationalism is rare and one is not always being told about virtues that one likes to discover for oneself: where, almost alone in the world today, the variety of tastes and opinions, the entrancing *variety* of the world is still encouraged and respected. People, I thought longingly, who when they go about are able here and there to care for other and different people as much as for their own. Perhaps it is only the best of any nation that can do this, and when we owned much of the world we often sent our best: but I was not thinking of being fair in the darkness of the night. The flint, I thought, is fire and the pebble mere stone: and people are civilized when *ideas*, however foreign, will strike a spark inside them: and England is now perhaps among those rare and happy nations where the fierce intellectual qualities of Greece have been toned down to a native goodness like the Turkish – a mixture that could produce civilization. If that is so, it is the treasure of treasures – and better to be conquered having it than to lack it among the threatening barbarians of our day.

Perseus in the Wind

Essays 1947

Who can say in what remoteness of time, in what difference of earthly shape, love first came to us as a stranger in the jungle? We, in our human family, know him through dependence in childhood, through possession in youth, through sorrow and loss in their season. In childhood we are happy to receive; it is the first opening of love. In youth we take and give, dedicate and possess – rapture and anguish are mingled, until parenthood brings a dedication that, to be happy, must ask for no return. All these are new horizons of content, which the lust of holding, the enemy of love, slowly contaminates. Loss, sorrow and separation come, sickness and death; possession, that tormented us, is nothing in our hands; it vanishes. Love's elusive enchantment, his ubiquitous presence, again become apparent; and in age we may reach a haven that asking for nothing knows how to enjoy.

• • •

One of the more charming Muhammedan saints walked always barefoot out of respect for earth, the carpet of God.

• • •

Religion is all an adventure in courage, and superstition a print of adventuring footsteps in the past, though it is apt to become more coercive than a footprint and to freeze, if it can, the exploring spirit from which itself was born. That, I imagine, is why the mystic is inclined to retreat from the habitations of man; to seek a world where every object he sees is not wound in a cocoon of thought and images created by others. He needs to get away from all these voices, he needs a footstool for meditation, and to watch, in the silence of his own heart, for the trail which so many wayfarers have confused. The true call of the desert, of the mountains, or the sea, is their silence – free of the network of dead speech. This silence without which

203

no enduring progress can be built must enter into all education that is worthy of the name.

❖   ❖   ❖

I remember one time on Mount Carmel, when in the sunset the sea was dove-grey, with a rosy light like the neck of a dove. From my stony height it looked burnished with innumerable ridges, but flat and wide so that Beato Angelico could have made angels walk there with hems lightly lifted, into the dying furnace of the sun. The sky was green jade, very pale; and there were clouds grey and white, the colour of ashes, and a slim moon, translucent as the wax of candles burning, and spanned as a thin eyebrow, or tartar bow. All these things were subdued, except the evening star; and that shone, not gold, but like an alloy of brass and silver and with its pale light stood in the van of the shadows of dusk.

❖   ❖   ❖

Who dares to be intellectual in the presence of death?

❖   ❖   ❖

The secret joy of peril comes from the veiled presence, without which most savour goes; and this is no morbid feeling, for the ecstasy belongs not to death in itself, but to *life*, suddenly enriched to know itself alive. So, after a summer dawn and climb till noon, among clefts and icy triangles or wind-scooped crannies, the mountaineer returning sets foot again on the short turf and flowers; and the breeze that cools him is the same breeze that sways the harebells; the blood that tramples in his ears and runs like chariots through his veins is the kind, swift, temporary stuff by which the smaller things of earth are fed; he is back in the community of his kind and descends, light-footed, among the pastures; but he remembers how in the high silences he has known himself on the edge of Silence and how its wing has brushed him. Once, looking down into a valley of the Lebanon, I have heard below

204

me as it were a swish of silk and seen, within a pebble's drop, an eagle's wings outspread; and so we watch death's flight, in our sunlight.

❖   ❖   ❖

The artist's business is to take sorrow when it comes. The depth and capacity of his reception is the measure of his art; and when he turns his back on his own suffering, he denies the very laws of his being and closes the door on everything that can ever make him great.

❖   ❖   ❖

Service became the instrument not only of Christianity but of every religion in the world, long before houses or housemaids were invented. It was the rose in the first desert, and still makes life possible for nurses, government officials, men in offices, whose work might otherwise be arid beyond their capacity to bear. It endows humble people with their chance of the greatest of worldly luxuries, since it makes of their labour, which is the only commodity they have, a thing that can be given. And it is free from the dangers of philanthrophy, since it is free from arrogance. Its secret of happiness is made manifest in any crisis, when men forget to care about their rights and think of service only.

It is, however, a two-sided virtue, not – like Love its begetter – a 'native of the rocks' and master of men. It needs a receiver as well as a giver and thrives on some small meed of welcome and honour; it is founded on co-operation. Not so long ago, a chit was circulated through government offices, begging them to recollect that 'the member of another department is not necessarily an enemy'. Bureaucracy, one fears, believes in economic man and is apt, by so doing, to despise service, having forgotten not so much to give as to receive.

❖   ❖   ❖

Among the peoples of the world memories held in common, that build themselves like coral islands from generation to generation, create a barrier of nationalism: for what is there in human beings to differentiate one from another in their essential qualities except their past? Like the words of their speech, the flags of nations go by heavy with encrusted meanings, the dust and stains of battlefields whose history is forgotten though the marks remain; they hang in the cathedrals of their people, whom they stir because of these old rents of war; and a new flag speaks as little as a new-coined word to the heart.

❖   ❖   ❖

Nationalism is a cutting and dividing virtue; people are frozen there in the shadow of collective adjectives, whose truth or falsehood is rarely brought home to them, and in any case seems remotely related to efforts of their own. But if one thing is more certain than another it is that the human soul is not collective; and the skeletons of Belsen show what happens when it tries to become so. The planner's shadow, perhaps efficient with external things, falls like death on the realms of the spirit where man the hand-made article, not mass-produced, stands on his feet alone.

❖   ❖   ❖

Nearly every manufactured thing that we handle is an extra to the necessities of life, whose natural bareness one has only to be a prisoner or a desert traveller to remember. We have spent all our history in complicating this essential simplicity: and sometimes I take in my hands some common object, a cup or kerchief or a reel of thread, and think of it in terms of the lives that have elaborated it and brought it through to us, until its homely familiar outlines grow majestic in the mere pyramid of time. The things used day by day and left by chance prove the steps of the human journey, like a lantern flickering by night that lurches in darkness and disappears and re-emerges, and shows where the invisible pathway runs.

❖ ❖ ❖

Very few things are dull in their universal setting: the loss of their abiding perspective makes the monotony.

❖ ❖ ❖

In a night of the month of April, the Arabs say that the oysters rise from their beds and float on the surface of the sea; and open their ragged shaly lips to collect a dew-drop as it falls; and so, having been united with heaven, descend again; and in the dim opaque twilight of their existence work their pearl round the heavenly core and build it with shining skins of light, one upon the other immeasurably fine, which the merchant later peels off at his pleasure, and stops where he pleases, when he is satisfied with the sheen of his jewel: for to that central dew-drop, invisible to men, no creature engaged in earthly commerce need trouble to attain. But the pearl will be more or less valuable according to the merchant's peeling, and he will hold it up for pleasure in his long slim Arab hand and wrap it in a shred of red velvet and bear it in his bosom, until he finds someone to buy it and carry it abroad, and hang it perhaps round the neck of folly, or possibly in the ear of kings.

❖ ❖ ❖

Beauty walks along the edge of opposites, between pattern and freedom. If pattern is too strong, the play of fancy ceases, and beauty with it; we foster rigid fashion and imitative arts. If freedom swings too wide we are lost in air.

❖ ❖ ❖

New Paphos itself is a dull and orphaned shore, more reminiscent of the landing of St. Paul, and of the toil and

207

disappointments of life, than of the Mother of Gods and
men. Aphrodite, however, did not land exactly there but
at a place a little farther to the east, called White Rocks,
where the remains of a temple are on a headland, above
a bay of polished boulders and white sand.

Here the long waves still lift their backs as if they
carried the queen of the world, and come in ranks with a
space between them, regiments saluting, with the morning
shining through the pennants and the plumes, the tossing
spray. The water has the gem-like lucidity of the Levant
and shows every pebble clean-cut through the advancing
wave. There are no trees about, but the swelling shapes of
grassy hills heavy with spicy odours in the sun; and a
simplicity, an absence of clefts or crannies, an openness
not cooled by shadows, but by the movements of the air
and water, the bare world rolling. Here someone, a shepherd or a seaman, saw Loveliness, and gave to the surrounding rocks for ever, to the sapphire horizon and the
whispering foam, the secret which the human being is
happy to know, perhaps only once – when he sees the eyes
of his beloved deeper than ocean and the Goddess herself
in their radiance, miraculous and alas! unembraceable as
the whiteness that bore her.

No creature can ever be derelict who has had this
moment. He is an initiate. He has seen the well of life
rising suddenly within its fleshly walls; out of the dark
unknown foundations of the world, emerging from chaos,
the glowing stream has risen stronger, more ancient, more
divine, than the sweet human form that contains it; and
the current has met above his being and carried him along
its dark perennial way.

⋄   ⋄   ⋄

We faced the wind that drops with the daylight, and
watched the throne of Olympus meet the sun. No mountain that I have seen has ever combined so much gentleness with its majesty, perhaps because it rises from so wide
a base, alone, and all the other summits in sight – south-

western Parnassus and eastern Athos, Ossa in the south and the opposite Balkan hills – have removed themselves in a wide arch, as if out of respect for the high public privacy of the gods, whose many-crested citadel, reared in a semicircle above the central gorge, shows from Ossa like a smooth tiara catching the morning light. The breadth of the summit, lifting to points as the top of a beduin tent lifts over the tent-poles, draws one's eye away from the steepness of cliff below. This great amplitude and serenity made me think of Zeus as he is pictured; the same unhindered majesty are in the words of Homer and in the mountain presence, and the hyacinth curls and broad untroubled forehead, the tranquil hand that holds the thunder, the immortal security that can partake of all life and never fear it – in some subtle manner the essence of these attributes seemed to reside in the aspect of Olympus. Its cliffs, rose-coloured and beguiling and dangerous as Aphrodite's fingers in the morning light, seemed to have lost their vertical striving; the horizontal lines of the great architecture held them. From our perch on Ossa we looked down into the Vale of Tempe, the river winding and the railway beside it and the mountain beyond; and felt the excitement of a genial world whose gods knew no heaven quite removed from the business of men.*

❖   ❖   ❖

Though beauty does not mean happiness, it is often found where happiness abides. And this, too, is strange about it and separates it from other qualities – that it is not recognized in a general fashion, but appears in different ways to all men, and differently even to the same man at different times. It comforts when all else fails in the house of sorrow, and breaks the silence there with its own more gentle silence, and soothes returning life into the limbs of pain. Plato thinks of it as a memory, seen fragmentarily and speaking to our hearts with sudden poignance of

* From 'Sunrise on Olympus', *London Magazine*, August 1955.

what they once have known. I am no philosopher and would not venture so deeply; yet I too, and nearly all human beings, I imagine, have felt that lightness as it were of recognition, which may be memory, or may also be, in the cosmic jigsaw, the sort of pleasure one has in finding two pieces that suddenly fit: they make no exact sense, but their joining brings us nearer to the understanding of the whole.

❖   ❖   ❖

When its . . . infancy was over, Memory began to take all human things, and warmed them and made them pliable as wax, and modelled them anew; altering the meaning of words and of banners, and the buildings of love; giving a value to pleasure and a halo to sorrow and joy. In the garment of memory man is encased like a grain of wheat in the sheaf of the ear, and the two are indistinguishable in the russet of the harvest.

❖   ❖   ❖

The drama of men is that their goodness creates, and their wickedness shatters, the goodness of others; so that pity holds us ever in leash, and there is no solitary road.

We set out, in the dawn of life gathering the tackle for our voyage, and soon leave the vessel of our elders and push our own craft to sea; and in strange ports gather new merchandise with opening eyes, and make with a steady or a wavering sail for the western stars: and on the high seas meet with traffickers and friends, and exchange our bales, and lift perhaps, to carry for someone in his shipwreck, the bundle of his treasure and his love. With our own goods we may traffic as we will; but what we take from another is dearer than our own, for we know not but it may be all the man has left him, and that his life may sink with it if we push it overboard; therefore we shall look carefully at what we take upon our decks, to see that it is indeed treasure and not nonsense, and – being sure of its value – carry it to the end.

❖   ❖   ❖

It would be well for us if sorrow came from magistrates and princes only. It is more deeply rooted. It stands in our landscape like the pyramids in Egypt whose shapes seem alien when first you see them with lengthening shadows across the fertile cultivation and burnished aisles of palms. The peasant walks in his slim thin gown along the dyke, with bare flat feet, and his buffaloes before him, and the shadows of these tyrants' monuments lie slanting across his way. There is no escape from them in the narrow way of civilization. And they have been seen so long across the panoramas of history, and have been gilded by so many sunsets that they come to be scarcely noticed, their human superfluous origin forgotten – the long agony of the building and lash of the contractor's whip; they are part of the surrounding desert and their sharp segments are never out of sight. And they are not unfriendly when they are looked at from flat roofs across the cotton fields in flower, in that hour when the smoke curls up from under the cooking-pot and children's voices lift in the air like bells, and the white ibis fly to their evening branches across the embers of the sky: there would be a blank and a strangeness if in the background of peaceful living the shapes of sorrow were nowhere to be seen.

❖   ❖   ❖

Civilizations do not degenerate through fear, but because they forget that fear exists.

❖   ❖   ❖

Hunger and love are favourable to life though surrounded by ruthlessness and danger, and therefore there is a human loyalty towards them. But with fear there is no truce. No taming, no hedge, no direction, can make

211

his way other than an evil way for men: he has no footprint that is not calamity: and all the triumph of a human
life is bound to his defeat.

❧ ❧ ❧

Fear, the oldest and perhaps the only enemy of man.

❧ ❧ ❧

There is much to be said for the English teaching,
which makes the whole aim of life a resistance to fear.
Even our smallest habits, our cultivation of discomforts,
our walking in all weathers and bathing in cold water, our
difficult spelling and monstrous weights and measures, our
draughty houses and rigorous cooking – are all a part of
the training to endure. And not in physical things only,
but in the disciplines of restraint and silence, of modesty
and the toleration of others, there is a protection of one's
identity under attack as it were, a strengthening of the
passive forms of courage, and a clearing of the ground
where it may grow: so that by specializing so much in
resistance we have become tough and quiet, courageous
but not militant, with a valour devoted to combat fear
and not to create it: and we are, I believe, as a nation
easier than most to live with in this world.

❧ ❧ ❧

The man who weeds is usually looked upon as innocent,
mild and harmless, an avoider of complexity, a lover of
peace, to whom the gentleness of nature opens when the
soil is moist and yielding and neither powdered with
drought nor sodden with rain. On such days, when the sun
finds woolly leaves that hold dew in shady corners, the
travelling bees and thin flies with straightlaced figures,
and beetles with hard metal business wings, and butterflies uncertain of their way come wandering through the
garden, each with an idea of his own as to what the defect
may be that divides the weeds and flowers. The true
gardener then brushes over the ground with slow and

212

gentle hand, to liberate a space for breath round some favourite; but he is not thinking about destruction except incidentally. It is only the amateur like myself who becomes obsessed and rejoices with a sadistic pleasure in weeds that are big and bad enough to pull, and at last, almost forgetting the flowers altogether, turns into a Reformer.

❖   ❖   ❖

The true secret of persuasiveness is that it *never* converts: it speaks to its own only, and discovers to them the unexpected secrets of their hearts.

❖   ❖   ❖

The rich start with a background of property marked 'Private', and are handicapped as givers. They forget that there are no possessions great enough to turn one from a debtor to a creditor in this world; the very beginning of gifts is the knowledge that all is one vast store, of which it is pleasant to hand something on, a cupful out of a flowing stream. They are apt to forget too that the tangible gifts are the smallest part of the store of human treasure. Beyond the enclosed reaches, the true giver comes again into the virgin forests of the Bhils, beside those rivers where use and need may dip: where receiving and giving are parts of a single action, a loveliness that grows like lilies in the coolness of a glade and, drawing all influences into its shining buds, scatters without effort the sweetness by which it lives.

❖   ❖   ❖

If I had to beg for my living I would rather do so in Asia than in Europe or America; not that Asiatic poverty is in itself more tolerable, but because they give a moral status to beggary there which the Reformation, or the Industrial Revolution, has long ago destroyed with us. The beggar in Asia, if the West has not yet touched him, comes up with no whine of servility; his 'looped and

213

windowed raggedness' is no stock-in-trade to awaken compassion, but is worn naturally; his hand is held out in a gesture of giving almost more than receiving; and when you have handed your coin, he refers you to Allah: 'Allah will repay,' as a young woman buying a hat might tell them to send the bill to her husband.

❖ ❖ ❖

The true giver gathers bounty and sheds it, knowing that it is but a part of what he and all men receive all the time.

❖ ❖ ❖

The quality of Passion; so direct, so fundamental, so naked and profound that formalists of all ages have spent the best part of their lives striving to iron it out of the souls of their pupils, denying its divine necessity and en-casing it in scaffoldings of behaviour whose transience they are at no pains to make manifest. And in the measure in which they succeed, our strength declines; like Antaeus, we lose contact with our earth, and our souls die; and it is quite a miracle that women, who have been brought up on the distortion of realities ever since the invention of petticoats, should still survive as normal beings, usually in exactly the degree in which they have been able to discard the teachings of their youth.

❖ ❖ ❖

Constancy, far from being a virtue, seems often to be the besetting sin of the human race, daughter of laziness and self-sufficiency, sister of sleep, the cause of most wars and practically all persecutions. We are for ever crystal-lizing, attempting to imprison what is fluid into a per-manent form. Religions are the most obvious examples – dams designed for eternity against the innate momentum of the human race. Their failure to petrify the natural inconstancy of man is made conspicuous by the greatness of the things with which they deal, but the story of any code or committee points the same moral.

❖   ❖   ❖

Marriage (as we are on the subject of permanent institutions) is too often a work of Art rather than Nature in this respect, a moment, so to say, frozen into permanence. Transitoriness it lamentably lacks; and the constancy which it exacts is sometimes inertia rather than fidelity. To combine marriage with a sense of insecurity, of the delightful fragility of earthly things, is surely desirable, and should be the effort of every intelligent husband or wife. Who would not be devoted to his wife if he knew she were to be beheaded next day? Men, being on the whole more intelligent and therefore by nature less constant than women, do frequently inspire a sense of insecurity, and by so doing obtain a far larger percentage of adoring partners. For if it is dull always to wish to look at the same picture, eat the same dinner, wear the same clothes, why should it not be so to want always the same person beside one? And if marriage is to be the apotheosis of Habit, then surely it is a form of death. The remedy is at hand, for it is not necessary to break up a home to find variety and change; to need it so tangibly means an unimaginative self or a dull partner, and the average man or woman has enough surprises to last a married life. But the cultivation of surprise must be regarded with due honour; monotony is not to be worshipped as a virtue; nor the marriage bed treated as a coffin for security rather than a couch from which to rise refreshed.

❖   ❖   ❖

Female education, when you come to consider it, is fundamentally complicated because it has to provide simultaneously for two completely different modes of life. From the beginning of Vanity, whenever that may be, till well into her middle age, a woman requires accomplishments different from – indeed, almost opposite to –

215

those which will make her old age happy. Between these conflicting divisions of her life, her mentors have oscillated since the beginning of time. It is only in Ages of Reason (and how few and unattractive they are) that the same virtues and accomplishments will carry her right through.

❖   ❖   ❖

The fallacy of our age maintains it better to do things badly than not at all. As a matter of fact there is very little harm in doing nothing: to do things badly is an active getting in the way of the few necessary people who might do good.

❖   ❖   ❖

Of the general inadequacy of intellect in the conduct of life Britain is the most majestic exponent.

❖   ❖   ❖

We are a people teetotal about thinking, whatever we may be about drink; and the idea of leisure in obscurity, with *thought* for enjoyment, makes no very general appeal.

❖   ❖   ❖

One of the pleasant things among the Arabs is their recognition of silence as a part of human intercourse: they sit round in a large gathering and, when the formal greetings and inquiries after health or absent friends are over, they let the minutes pass, two, four, ten minutes, in meditation, until someone takes an idea and throws it like a stone into the middle of a pond, where all have time to watch its ripples spread.

❖   ❖   ❖

Neither Shakespeare nor any other magician can ever utter the whole truth, or even express what he really means to say. This penalty was laid on human speech when or before the tower of Babel stood: perhaps it produced the germ of discontent in Eden. Every later revolu-

216

tion in history is the record of human efforts to keep words and their meaning as nearly together as they can, for the quality of civilization depends on the calling of things by their proper names as far as we can know them.

❖ ❖ ❖

Anyone who tries to write knows that there is not the simplest most tangible thing in existence that can be described entire. The roots of all go down uncharted, like sea rocks whose wizened surface the smallest waves lick over – though great mountains and submarine valleys may underlie them, with monsters or mermaids in their depths. All this and more, to the very centre of earth and extremity of time, is part of their truth; and the task of every statement or description is to decide how much of it all is to be included. As a rule, we are satisfied with a surface verity and say of these rocks that they are bleached or dry or sharp or rounded, ignoring and even contradicting the foundations on which they stand: but those who possess the secret of words are able as it were to pack the meaning, and fill it with greater space and wider time, so that a more capacious quality of truth is implicit in the things they say.

❖ ❖ ❖

Accuracy is the basis of style. Words dress our thoughts and should fit; and should fit not only in their utterances, but in their implications, their sequences, and their silences, just as in architecture the empty spaces are as important as those that are filled. The problem of all writing is the same as that presented by the composition of a telegram, one has to convey a meaning with the use of few and always inadequate words, and eke it out with what the reader, drawing upon his own reserves, will understand. The number of words that even the most profuse writer will dare to use is always insufficient for a complete impression, but the reserves he can draw upon in the reader's mind are lavish indeed. The whole generalship

217

of writing is in the summoning and marshalling of these unseen auxiliaries.

This necessary co-operation makes tradition in literature valuable – the gradual development of a vast familiar field. It also makes it difficult to acquire a 'style' in a foreign language, where the writer must rely on his own words merely and has few or none of the subtleties of his readers' background to play with. It is as if a musician were condemned to have the resonance taken out of his notes.*

❦   ❦   ❦

Style is fundamentally a truthful statement, if we take for truth something more careful than the not telling of a lie. There are layers and layers of truth; and style, whether in dress or life, art or literature, is involved in their discovery.

In the matter of dress, for instance, how profoundly justified is the scorn that every wise woman feels for the word 'utility' and all that it implies. Utility, like charity, is not puffed up; it vaunteth not itself; it is comparatively innocent, and does not make of its victims aliens to their own selves, which is active falsehood and bad taste and a pitfall to the unwary who think expense and fashion are enough. Utility is not unseemly. But it seeks to avoid offence in a dull, negative way by discovering an average in human needs and the average is dowdy. Now truth is *never* average. Since there is not one single thing in the world exactly like another, the very essence of truth is that it leaps across averages to the particular, at any rate as far as anything is concerned that we are likely to have to deal with on this earth: and therefore Woman, who is primitive and deals with ultimate facts, will do the best she can to particularize her utility into some trick, some shape, some detail, which fits her own surroundings and herself. To her men she appears infatuated by singularity – and we may admit that there are moments of excess –

* From 'Saying What One Means', B.B.C. Talk, July 21, 1962.

but at her best it is herself that she is trying to discover; and if she or her dressmaker succeed, she achieves the secret of style in her clothes.

⋄ ⋄ ⋄

The figures stand round the crowned dancing girl in a formal group, full of courtly awareness, neither pressing nor yielding, and the artist – practised in the world's way – has given care to the gorgeous detail of each garment, to the collars of threaded gems, to the expensive veil that lies upon the wrist with such accomplished lightness, to the badges of rank – strange lozenge patches – laid on the long mantles of the nobles. In every fold of the elaborate straight gowns, in the cold breeding of the eyes and hands and their languid treacherous repose, in the air of easy courtier respect that surrounds the empress who smoulders wilful and dangerous, encrusted with jewels and gold; in that lady-in-waiting, subservient and arrogant, so exquisitely maided, so cruelly sure of power – there is as it were a heightening of meaning, an electric charge of something that the actual ingredients of the picture are in themselves insufficient to explain.*

It seems to me that one might define this heightening of meaning as *style*.

⋄ ⋄ ⋄

Terrible or tragic history is not necessary for the production of greatness in art; the faintest summer breath holds melodies and dirges enough if genius happens to be listening. But results even then are in close relation to the weight of the feeling behind them, and it is possible that people are searched more deeply, the surface of life is pierced more frequently, and the stimulus is sharper in an age of conflict, than in those periods which we fallaciously think of as secure. Nothing here is secure, and in this certainty the future of art lies safe.

⋄ ⋄ ⋄

* Tomb of Empress Theodora in San Vitale, Ravenna.

219

It is lucky to live in a city on a hill and to be saved by the view at one's window from thinking of the world as flat, so that one may see at a glance how all we have in sight slips over some edge into the veils of space.

❖　❖　❖

Though it may be unessential to the imagination, travel is necessary to an understanding of men. Only with long experience and the opening of his wares on many a beach where his language is not spoken, will the merchant come to know the worth of what he carries, and what is parochial and what is universal in his choice. Such delicate goods as justice, love and honour, courtesy, and indeed all the things we care for, are valid everywhere; but they are variously moulded and often differently handled, and sometimes nearly unrecognizable if you meet them in a foreign land; and the art of learning fundamental common values is perhaps the greatest gain of travel to those who wish to live at ease among their fellows.

❖　❖　❖

A dignity unattainable even to the gods is given to mortal things by the mere fact of their mortality. The gaiety of young men going to battle, the mellowness of crumbling walls, the grace of flowers, the delicacy of age, all fragilities glow as it were in the light of their own annihilation; the transient world gets its nobility from the very heart of its weakness, and the lights and shadows are thrown by that vision of darkness which closes on blossoming days.

So it is with histories of nations. In the pages of Gibbon we read with a heightened emotion the least petty gossip of Constantinople as the Ottomans advance upon it; we follow the daily life of Rome with Attila already in the north, and study with the same poignancy many a nearer record of our day. To the heart's eye no visible catastrophe is needed; the ways we are brought up in, our fashions, fetishes, and hopes, also pass to their exits and gain dignity as we realize how temporary they are. And here lies the charm of Arab travel. We visit something that has vanished from our West long ago, and in the East can linger but a short while longer. It is this unconscious background of catastrophe which lures us to the beduin of the desert rather than to the modern Effendi who lives in towns like ours and shares our future, whose transitory nature is as yet unapparent. In the desert life, in so much of the Eastern world, every detail counts because it may never be repeated: even the most casual traveller must feel that the light he strikes is much more important, because not one but two eternities, the past and the future, are waiting to engulf it.*

❖   ❖   ❖

There is this about love: that its memory is not enough: for the soul retracts if it does not go on loving, whereas to have travelled once, however long ago – provided it was real and not bogus travel – is enough.

❖   ❖   ❖

It is February, and raining – a cold spring rain. In the Dolomites, behind mists and foothills this rain is snow; the hesitating flakes, whiter than the sky that produces them, are falling on uninhabited places, or on pastures only visited in summer; they press, like the lives of men, thick and gentle, out of a blankness teeming with their numbers, and cover each other with oblivion. If they make a sound at all, it is some tiny crackle of crystal layers, imperceptible as our world's noises to a star. They have no memory of the clouds and dews and the sources from which they come. They are wound into the stuff of the world, and their familiar outline is sharp only because darkness surrounds it, as the harmony of words or music flowers out of silence.

❖   ❖   ❖

* From the Foreword to *Arabia Phoenix* by Gerald de Gaury, 1948.

Some words come heavily jewelled out of their history. Feelings and thoughts have been encrusted on them in their passage through centuries and nations, and Oxus

Rejoicing, through the hush'd Chorasmian waste
Under the solitary moon

carries a siren magic; there is, as it were, a patina of old bronze produced by use and time. This jewelled quality of language gives richness to literature. It gives to words the same atmosphere that a house acquires by being loved and lived in – whose magnificence is not expressed but latent, and belongs neither to the builder nor to the present user of the dwelling; but has been gathered unconsciously by those who, in careless generations, have played and used and left the mark of their lives upon their symbols.

❖   ❖   ❖

Pictures of one's childhood are as fragmentary as the relics of the sailor's way which wanders through the south of England; a stretch emerges here and there, though most of it has vanished or been transformed. Amid these half-obliterated memories I can see, quite sharply, my first meeting with the image of death.

I must have been about four years old and a nurse in our grandmother's house was putting me to bed. It was a Victorian house where fireplaces had tall brass fenders highly polished, and the black metal bed-rails ended in knobs of brass; many pillows, beginning with bolsters, were piled up towards a chintz canopy from which curtains descended, securely lined against draughts, tied with tasselled ropes of red and green. Standing there on the eiderdown, being buttoned into a long nightgown that lay about my feet, I asked if my mother would live for ever.

'No,' said nurse, 'not for ever; but for a long time.'

'How long?' said I. 'A thousand years?'

'No,' said nurse. 'Not a thousand years.'

The finality of Time was borne in upon me. Hours afterwards my parents, coming up to bed, found me half asleep but still sobbing at the top of the stairs, where I had crept a little nearer to those dear ones who in a thousand years would be dead.

This feeling has never really changed. If the world is not to last for ever, it seems to make no difference whether its time is to be counted in millions or billions of years; what matters is that there is an end. There can be no safe happiness until the fact has been faced and assimilated; and an absolute condition of all successful living, whether for an individual or a nation, is the acceptance of death.

⬦　⬦　⬦

Good days are to be gathered like sunshine in grapes, to be trodden and bottled into wine and kept for age to sip at ease beside his fire. If the traveller has vintaged well he need trouble to wander no longer; the ruby moments glow in his glass at will. He can still feel the spring in his step, and the wind on his face, though he sit in shelter: unless perhaps the sight of a long road winding, or the singing of the telegraph wires, or the wild duck in their wedges, or horses' hooves that clatter into distance, or the wayside stream – all with their many voices persuade him to try just one more journey before the pleasant world comes to an end.

⬦　⬦　⬦

On the whole, age comes most gently to those who have some doorway into an abstract world – art, or philosophy, or learning – regions where the years are scarcely noticed and young and old can meet in a pale truthful light. We move there with increasing freedom as Time rubs out the illusions of possession, whose dark attendant, envy, fades away. The loss of our own things, or such we thought so, our faculties, our friends, our loves – makes us again receptive as in childhood, though now it is no human hand that gives. In our increasing poverty, the universal riches grow more apparent, the careless showering of gifts

223

regardless of return; our private grasp lessens, and leaves us heirs to infinite loves in a common world where every joy is a part of one's personal joy. With a loosening hold returning towards acceptance, we prepare in the ante-room for a darkness where even this last personal flicker fades, and what happens will be in the Giver's hand alone.

❖   ❖   ❖

This is the prospect from the watershed, and when the traveller reaches it, it is a good thing to take an hour's leisure and look out on the visible portions of the journey, since never in one's life can one see the same view twice. I have placed my bundle beside me and found a flat stone and settled in the sun with my back to the road of my coming, and have looked as far as I can into the valley where the track is lost. And as the eye soon tires with so little detail to hold it, and the mist wreathes all in its timeless festoons, and no mortal inn is in sight – I have opened my bundle and sorted the few things collected and carried through the morning's climb, to count what personal oddments are there to help me on my way. This little book is the list of these things; and as it is a random assortment, not harvested from learning but from life and accident, it is probably just like the list of millions of other travellers, since the journey we make is the same. Who asks for originality in a soldier's kit-bag, or the knapsack of a mountaineer? Or who would not think it presumptuous in the snowflake to wish to be unique in its manner of falling to the ground? My hope is the very opposite; for we are all – unless suddenly cut off – bound to grow old; and as I am fortunate in looking to old age without either misgiving or regret, but with an interest of travel – I like to think that these stray reflections may not have been written for myself only, but for all who have climbed and crossed their ridges and are standing with me upon the verge of afternoon.